Building Your Life Skills

Inspiring, informative books for thoughtful readers wanting to make changes and realise their potential.

Other **Pathways** books include:

Getting Your Next Job
A systematic approach to find the career
that is best for you

Healing the Hurt Within
Understand and relieve the suffering
behind self-destructive behaviour

Women Returning to Work
How to work out what you
want and then go out and get it

Please send for a free copy of the catalogue for full details
(see back cover for address).

Building Your
Life Skills

*Who are you, where are you, and where do
you want to go: a personal action plan*

Judith Johnstone

PATHWAYS

First published in 1999 by
How To Books Ltd., 3 Newtec Place,
Magdalen Road, Oxford OX4 1RE, United Kingdom
Tel: 01865 793806   Fax: 01865 248780

British Library Cataloguing in Publication Data
A catalogue record for this book is available from
the British Library

Editing by Barbara Massam   Cover image PhotoDisc
Cover design by Shireen Nathoo Design

Produced for How To Books by Deer Park Productions
Typeset by Euroset, Alresford, Hampshire SO24 9PQ
Printed and bound in Great Britain

Note: The material contained in this book is set out in good
faith for general guidance and no liability can be accepted for
loss or expense incurred as a result of relying in particular
circumstances on statements made in the book. The laws and
regulations are complex and liable to change, and readers
should check the current position with the relevant
authorities before making personal arrangements.

Pathways is an imprint of
How To Books

Contents

List of Worksheets

Preface

Why do you need to build up your life skills? What's in it for you if you do?

Life skills can be thought of as a life raft. Each skill is a separate plank to help you keep afloat no matter where you are on the sea of life. And as most of us come to realise at quite an early stage, our journey on the sea of life is not always plain sailing. So anything which can keep us buoyed up instead of bogged down – or even prevent us from sinking – is something we should be exploring very seriously.

Just look at the changes which have taken place in the UK over the past ten years in the workplace, in our lifestyles and in the increasing number of people living to a ripe old age.

Changes in the work scene have been momentous and far-reaching. The unprecedented drop in the number of unskilled and semi-skilled jobs is just one example. There has been a dramatic shift away from once traditional manufacturing industries which employed thousands of people. In their place service industries have mushroomed, needing a very different range of skills and competencies. Computerised systems have invaded practically every workplace. There are more part-time jobs and short-term contracts than ever before. The emphasis is increasingly on multi-skilling and adaptability to change. Having educational qualifications alone is no longer enough to ensure employability: skill has become as important as academic know-how.

The workforce has changed too. Some employers have deliberately introduced early retirement as part of their drive to cut wage bills. Many middle-managers, predominantly men in their forties and fifties, have suddenly found themselves 'retired', voluntarily or otherwise. At the same time, the increasing number of part-time jobs have appealed to women wanting to earn money while still retaining their more traditional family roles. More women than ever before are now part of the workforce – around

50 per cent and still rising. But not everyone wants part-time employment. There are signs that more and more people are having to seriously consider taking on two or more part-time jobs to make ends meet. Others are having to come to terms with the loss of what used to be taken for granted – a job for life – and are facing the need to start from scratch with a new career.

Our lifestyles have changed too: the increasing number of single parents and marriage breakdowns; fewer marriages taking place; many women deferring starting their families until their late thirties, and the steady rise in the number of people living well into their eighties and nineties. In twenty years or so it is quite likely that medical advances will increase everyone's chances of reaching 100. Consequently, more and more of us in the future are likely to find we are the third generation in our family who are no longer part of the working population. For some people it is a sobering thought that if you 'retire' at 50 with the potential of becoming a centenarian, half your life lies beyond the world of work.

If you look at what constitutes 'a working life' nowadays, it already represents only around 40 per cent of the average lifespan. Concentrating on work skills alone therefore, which is the latest popular credo, is not particularly helpful. The study of life skills is not just about skills for work, but *for life*.

So, if you are searching for better job prospects or wanting to return to work; keen to make better use of your home life or spare time; seeking personal development in difficult circumstances, or looking for more fulfilment in retirement, this book is for you. By suggesting ways of looking at your life and achievements so far, combined with a process of self-assessment, it will help you identify what skills you already have (and you may be surprised by how many there are); those you need to revitalise or build on; which new ones you should acquire, and what other skills you might like to have simply for the personal satisfaction they would give you. It will be an exhilarating and rewarding voyage of discovery. Enjoy it.

Judith Johnstone

Acknowledgements

My thanks to the Department for Education and Employment Manchester for the summary of *The Learning Age*; Arabella Woods of the DfEE Library in London for historical data on the introduction and workings of the Certificate of Secondary Education; Roy Harrison of the Institute of Personnel and Development for the Welsh Office document *Learning is for Everyone* and for the IPD response to it; the organisation Cumbria Enterprise, who as Cumbria TEC in 1993 invited me to a seminar on ' New Horizons for Women' which introduced me to the concept of competencies in the home and in unpaid voluntary work; Val Halbert of the Centre for Continuing Education, Training and Development at Lancaster University for providing details of current NVQs on offer at the Centre; The University for the Third Age for background material; Andy Jones, Head of Sixth at Keswick School who asked me to produce course notes and worksheets for Year 12 students on the topic of life skills which I have been able to incorporate in part into this book; and last but not least the hundred or so Year 12 students themselves who tested the course content and provided me with such stimulating and rewarding responses to the ideas put to them.

JJ

The fault ... is not in our stars, But in ourselves, that we are underlings.
SHAKESPEARE: JULIUS CAESAR

Giving Yourself Credit

K nowledge of your life skills is going to affect how you see yourself in several ways. It will:

◆ help you cope with the rough patches in your life;
◆ improve your self-confidence through self-awareness;
◆ provide signposts for an alternative lifestyle;

and probably most important of all, it will

◆ transform *change* in your life into *challenge*.

> We all have more skills than we give ourselves credit for.

There are all sorts of reasons why we tend to hide our lights under convenient bushels. In some circumstances we don't like to give the impression we are boasting or trying to sound too pushy. In others we take a conscious decision not to acknowledge our abilities, either because we feel it is inappropriate under the prevailing circumstances, or because it could damage a comfortable status quo we don't want to be responsible for destroying. At other times our reticence is entirely unintentional: we simply overlook what we can do or what we are capable of, discounting something either because we take it for granted or because it just never enters our heads since the ability is so commonplace.

This tendency to think ourselves less than we are can have the effect of becoming a self-fulfilling prophecy. Negative thoughts produce negative results. If we are underlings, then the problem does not lie with the heavy hand of Fate, but in our own unwillingness to acknowledge we can do so much more with our lives if we make the effort.

In Chapters 1 to 5 we will be unearthing your hidden talents and setting up skills audits. Chapters 6 to 10 will be looking at the many and varied ways of using these skills in different circumstances.

So let's begin by throwing off any artificial coyness or preconceived ideas about what we should or should not recognise as a 'skill' and begin this exploration with a sense of curiosity and a thirst for knowledge.

Preparing the groundwork

To use the analogy of an expedition as an illustrative tool for a little longer, planning the process of discovering your skills will depend on whether your journey is purely for pleasure – out of curiosity perhaps, or for a more serious purpose – to change your life. How you use the ideas suggested in this book is entirely up to you: you can skim the contents from start to finish; mull over parts you feel are more applicable to yourself; study the worksheets and questionnaires as pieces of continuous project work, or come back to the task over a period of time. Naturally, the more you think about the questions raised and search for the answers, the more you will get from the experience.

Setting up base camp

The journey you are about to start is a reflective experience. It is not something you will find easy to do in a busy or noisy environment. You will need to set aside at least a small corner for your personal space where you can be left undisturbed for an hour or so at a time. Those around you will also need to be understanding and prepared to give you this freedom.

Of course, not everyone is in a position to control the activities of those around them. You may be sharing a flat with several other free spirits who enjoy mega-bass music; you may be a fond parent of a young and boisterous brood, or someone caring for an elderly relative who enjoys 24-hour TV. If finding a place of sanctuary where you can apply yourself to the task for a reasonable length of time is almost impossible, the answer is to do what you can when you can: read on a bus or train; buy some inexpensive earplugs (soft spongy ones are just the job), or adopt counter measures by wearing headphones and listening to your personal choice of music to muse by.

Recording your findings

Like any good explorer, adventurer or traveller, you will want some means of recording what you find on your journey. To do this you will need:

◆ a robust A4 ring binder or lever arch file;
◆ a small pocket-sized note pad for brainstorming ideas when away from base camp;
◆ a cheap pad of rough paper for draft work;
◆ a good quality A4 lined paper pad, or printer paper if you intend to type or word-process the finished product;
◆ a supply of anti-static clear plastic multipunched pockets to protect certificates, newspaper cuttings, letters etc;
◆ a selection of pens, pencils, highlighters etc. to suit your work style.

The worksheets you will find in this book are suggested layouts only, for you to copy and adapt as you choose. Because everyone's life experiences are different, prescribing the amount of space you should take over recording your particular piece of history is not very helpful. Make it as long or as short as it needs to be. The same is true of the self-assessment questionnaires to identify your skills; the memory joggers to remind you of people, places and events which have helped to shape your life, and the thinking slots designed to stimulate self-awareness. What is important is that your record is as comprehensive and complete as possible, and precisely because it is for your eyes only, you should be totally honest with yourself when you are working on it.

From now on this record is going to be referred to as your Personal Resource Pack, or PRP for short.

> You should think of your Personal Resource Pack as a one-stop reference point.

Once you have completed the worksheet, self-assessment questionnaire, memory jogger and thinking slot data you need to include in it, it should provide you with a first-class tool to use over and over again.

Like most travel journals your PRP should be thought of as a continuing process, like your journey through life itself. So don't treat your PRP documentation as a work of art to be finished, perhaps touched up once or twice and then put to one side to be admired occasionally. Think of it as an extension of yourself.

◆   Add to it if you've forgotten something earlier.
◆   Extend it if you feel you've something important you should include that hasn't been accounted for.
◆   Redesign it, if a slightly different format suits you better, or you want to put the whole thing onto disk.

But whatever else you do, there are two very important pieces of guidance to follow:

---

1   Keep it up to date.
2   Keep it with other records of achievement you may already have, or better still, amalgamate them.

What you then have at your finger tips is a handy reference work with everything you need to have in one place. This is especially useful if you want to

◆   use it to complete application forms;
◆   extract data to compile your curriculum vitae (CV);
◆   plan what you would like to do in the future; or
◆   have a starting point for developing a record of your continuous professional or personal development.

But probably the most important role for your Personal Resource Pack is to use it when you feel you need a welcome morale booster. If you don't know where to turn for inspiration – or worse, if life is just getting you down –

◆   read and reread it to remind yourself of your range of skills and achievements.

You will find this is the best tonic or instant pick-you-up you could ever give yourself – and it doesn't leave you with a hangover.

Setting aside some time

Your journey will take as long as you want it to and a lot depends on the reasons you have for setting out in the first place. You may not feel the need to delve too deeply into certain aspects en route, or you may be looking for every clue or signpost along the way to help you make a decision about your next move. The route itself has been planned for you by the layout of this book, so some of the hard work has already been done. The rest is up to you.

If there is one piece of advice which it is really important to give you right at the start it is – give yourself plenty of time to think. The quality and value of what you discover about yourself will depend on this to a very large extent. So follow these simple rules:

1 Think about what you are being asked to consider.
2 Let ideas roll around freely in your head for a while.
3 Jot down answers as soon as they come to mind.

And most important of all:

4 Don't under any circumstances discount or cross out anything because on reflection you think it is irrelevant.

The written word is a powerful tool: it doesn't disappear with the next brain impulse to be overlaid by new thoughts, or float away on the air to be lost for ever like so much of the spoken word. It sits there on the page telling you something, nagging at you to take notice of it. So do just that.

Recognising your skills and abilities

Now you are prepared for your adventure, for the remainder of this chapter we will be looking at a whole range of skills and abilities we might possess. Some we are born with, others we acquire throughout our childhood, and still others are those we accrue or build on through experiences which come from many different inputs over the years.

To begin at the beginning: what is a skill?

> A skill is your ability to do something.

Skills come in all shapes and sizes. Many can be identified by breaking down tasks into descriptive action words such as *reading, organising, coordinating, advising, computing, copying, singing, dancing,* or similar *-ing* words. Others are physical skills such as *good hand-to-eye coordination, perfect tonal pitch, fast reflexes* for example, but they should not be confused with physical attributes such as being the heaviest, tallest, toughest, strongest, fastest: these are not skills. Then there are the social skills, such as being a *good* *listener, a good communicator* or *a good leader*. Others are skills which we have acquired through experience or by learning, or a combination of both linked with a natural ability, such as *an aptitude for languages* or *music, mathematical skills, IT skills* and so on.

Skills therefore are not limited to a narrow range of capabilities: they cover a very much wider sweep of our day-to-day activities. And because of this it is easy to overlook or discount some of the more obvious ones.

Introducing you to your range of skills and abilities

In this chapter you will not be completing any skills audits as such: Chapters 2 to 5 are devoted to these after exploring the main sources of your life skills in greater depth. However, you will find it useful to record your thoughts on the questions raised by the thinking slots in this chapter, even if only in the form of very rough notes to use as aides-mémoire later on. Keep these notes safe in either your ring binder or lever arch file.

The aim now is to get you into the right frame of mind to begin thinking in a slightly different way about yourself, particularly about how all the various experiences of your life have affected who you are and what you can do.

> Discovering your skills isn't just about the skills themselves, but what you have done with them, what you are doing with them and what you might do with them in the future.

Be prepared for some surprises.

Looking at subconscious skills

Many of the skills we have are at a purely subconscious or unconscious level: we do them automatically and without thinking. There are for example the most basic instinctive skills of *flight* or *fight*. As a species we have survived into the 21st century precisely because the majority of us have this inbuilt skill of self-preservation, or its more altruistic version, the preservation of the rest of the group.

Most of us in the West, however, do not need to survive at this level. Our culture and lifestyle have superimposed other, more sophisticated layers onto the most basic instinctive skills we possess. But although we may have become more sophisticated in some ways, there are still several physical skills we use as a matter of course which are 'basic' nonetheless.

Take an average morning event as an example. You are tucked up in bed asleep. The alarm clock rings and you wake up. You reach out and push down the alarm button. You pick up the clock and peer at it closely. Alas, it is time to get up. You climb out of bed, stumble bleerily to the bathroom , wash and dress and then head down to the kitchen to make breakfast and say 'good morning' to the dog.

Let's just stop there for a moment. Go back and reread the previous paragraph. As you do, ask yourself the following questions:

1   How would the above scenario differ if I were deaf?
2   How would it differ if I were blind?
3   How much of the above could I achieve if I were a paraplegic?
4   What would happen if I were a quadriplegic?

From your own personal experience you may already know the answer to one or more of these questions without any prompting. Anyone who is coping with any sort of disability knows only too well that often the simplest activities involve some of the skills which they do not possess – the basic skills associated with hearing, seeing, talking and touching.

So much of our everyday lives depends on these skills combining together in an unconscious way that we move around from one task to the next without a second thought. Good hand/ear coordination means we can pinpoint the location of the clock, even in the dark with our eyes closed. Good hand/eye coordination enables us to see the clock and pick it up to check the time. Good ear/eye functioning allows us to get out of bed and stand up without overbalancing and landing in a heap on the floor.

We don't just use these skills for the mundane tasks of everyday living, we employ them at work and at play as well. Just think for a moment about how many of these interrelated skills you use to take a phone message or play a ball game. More than you expected, no doubt.

Where do you stand in the foundation skills league?

Thinking Slot 1

- How would you describe your sight (unaided)?
  Good/Satisfactory/Poor/Non-existent
- How would you describe your hearing (unaided)?
  Good/Satisfactory/Poor/Non-existent
- Do you rely on some form of aid to improve your
  sight/hearing?
- How good is your sense of balance?
  Good/Satisfactory/Poor/Non-existent
- How would you describe your ability to speak? Good/Slightly
  impaired/Badly impaired/No speech
- How good is your sense of touch? Good/Satisfactory/Non-
  existent
- How good is your sense of taste? Good/Satisfactory/Non-
  existent
- How good is your sense of smell? Good/Satisfactory/Non-
  existent

Thinking about these foundation skills gives you some idea of
the extent of the base you are working from. If you have all your
faculties in full working order then, theoretically, the world is your
oyster.

But not having your faculties in full working order doesn't
mean you can't achieve, or that the skills you have should in any
way be regarded as second class. Far from it. Very often if you lose
one or more of your foundation skills, or they don't function
quite as well as they should, your remaining faculties help to make
up the deficiency. Total loss of sight can encourage a keener sense
of hearing and vice versa. And where the loss is accompanied by
additional physical difficulties, such as those which can be
experienced after a stroke or an accident, we are remarkably
proficient at adopting different strategies to achieve our ends. So
it is often the case that someone wrestling with a disability
develops alternative skills to overcome the problem. You only need
to look at some of the magnificent paintings completed by those
who use their mouths or feet instead of their hands to recognise
what can be achieved despite an acute physical disability.

If you have any form of disability or handicap, give some thought to the following.

Thinking Slot 2
- What is your disability or handicap?
- Have you developed any strategies to overcome this?
- What additional skills do you think you have developed as a result?
- What advantage do you think this might give you over an able-bodied person?

Basic learning skills

The three Rs have had a bumpy ride over the years, in and out of fashion until, rather like the hokey-cokey, they have been well and truly shaken all about. But regardless of what the latest educational guru teaching might be, being able to read, write and cope with simple mathematical problems remain the three skills most needed when we apply for a job. More importantly, they are all essential if we want to make sense of our lives. Anyone who has had to struggle with some form of dyslexia can testify to the frustrations and often the embarrassment of not being able to understand the basic structures of the written word or the mysterious concepts behind the manipulation of figures.

Numeracy

Numeracy at the simplest level comprises the ability to add, subtract, multiply and divide (without a calculator) and to understand what is happening when these processes take place.

Without this basic understanding even something as mundane as doing the household shopping can be traumatic and fraught with difficulties. If you cannot understand the amounts quoted on the side of a tin or packet, you have to guess whether the packaging looks as though it might hold enough for your purposes. The prices quoted on the label or the supermarket shelf are little more than meaningless symbols. Even if you are told how much something costs you are unlikely to be able to give the right money or check the change you are given.

Literacy

Literacy is the ability both to read and to write. To understand the written word and be able to use it in a meaningful way to provide information either to yourself or others is a powerful social tool.

Someone who has impaired sight but who can read (and write) in Braille has greater skills than their sighted counterpart: they have the additional ability of being able to translate raised matrix configurations on paper into meaningful words through a delicate sense of touch. This is another instance where disability involves the acquisition of a wider, more demanding range of skills.

Reading and writing are the most important of the basic skills you need today because there is very little in our modern lives which you can do without them. The days of illiterate agricultural and factory workers are long gone, and so are the manual jobs which went with them.

To return once more to the analogy of shopping as an illustration of how important these skills are – if you cannot write, you cannot make a list of items you need to buy; if you cannot read, you have to rely on the illustrations on packets and tins to give you some clue as to what the contents might be. And when you get your purchases home, you are at a loss as to how they should be cooked because you cannot understand the instructions, and even the simplest book of recipes is quite beyond your grasp.

Verbal communication

Verbal communication is the other side of the literacy coin. It is the ability to express your thoughts in a concise and precise way which is understandable to your listeners.

Like reading and writing, this too is a powerful social tool, one which predates reading and writing by many centuries. Oral histories and tradition were embedded in the social fabric of many societies long before the concept of writing, and can still be found in some parts of the more remote regions of the world today.

Verbal communication involves a complicated set of rules which string words together to convey meaning. How we acquire language is a fascinating topic in itself, a combination of what appears to be instinct refined by what we learn from others – a truly remarkable skill.

Those denied the power of speech, or the ability to hear speech, have evolved a series of expressive hand movements – sign language – another form of communication and very much a skill in its own right, as anyone who has tried to master its complexities will tell you – it is far from easy .

Skills from school and higher or further education

Without the basic skills discussed earlier we would not be able to achieve the broader range of abilities we learn during our years at school and beyond.

The curriculum in schools has changed quite dramatically since the Education Act of 1944. The merger of grammar and secondary modern schools to form comprehensives drew together the separate strands of academic and technical skills teaching. More recent changes mean children in today's schools are not just taking General Certificate of Secondary Education (GCSE) and Advanced Levels (A Levels) in the traditional academic subjects of Maths, English, the Sciences, Humanities and Languages, but also in the more technical subjects such as Electrical Systems and Computer Aided Design. There is also a new breed of qualifications – the General National Vocational Qualifications (GNVQs), where progress is measured according to the concept of *competence* – the ability to use a *skill* to a specified standard. Pupils taking GNVQs have a better understanding of how skills are used in the workplace and can relate much more easily to the National Vocational Qualifications (NVQs) which good employers use as training tools to improve the quality of their workforce.

In the last decade there has also been a tremendous upsurge in the use of Information Technology (IT) in the classroom, even at primary school level. Word processing is a presentational skill expected of students in producing coursework, so now many pupils are perfectly capable of designing documents, leaflets etc. which would have been the province of printers and graphic designers only a few short years ago.

> Computer literacy in the young has left many parents feeling they might be living on another planet.

IT is now a core skill embedded in the subjects taught by schools. This is common sense when you consider how much the computer has already invaded the workplace, and access to the internet promises to become as commonplace as the TV in the average home in the not so distant future.

Another change to the curriculum has been the emphasis on language acquisition, not just English but at least one foreign language. Language skills have increasingly come to the fore as a result of our gradual integration into the European Union. For those with the ability to absorb a foreign language there are many more opportunities available today both in the workplace and at a social level.

At college or university, educational skills expand into a new dimension: they move away from fundamental knowledge and simplistic questioning into more complex evaluation and analysis of subject matter. Here are a new range of skills drawing on abilities to set out hypotheses, carry out research or experimentation, analyse and question results, and finally to come to well-reasoned sustainable conclusions.

Pause here and consider the following questions.

Thinking Slot 3

- How would you describe your educational skills?
  - Basic
  - Secondary
  - Higher
- Would you like to improve them?
- How would you like to improve them?

Skills in the workplace

Occupational skills are many and varied. They can be put into broad categories and then divided and subdivided right down to the simplest action involved. It is not the aim of this chapter to go through this process now because this is to be looked at in much greater detail in Chapter 3 when you will be concentrating on your own skills. In the meantime, however, it will be worthwhile getting the flavour of what is to come and to start mulling over some of the ideas explored here.

Types of skill

Occupations are often divided into broad general categories. We meet them in circumstances where occupational data is being collected, such as in the ten-yearly National Census, or market research. Here are some examples of occupational categories:

- Managerial
- Professional
- Administrative
- Clerical and secretarial
- Security and protection services
- Skilled trades
- Personal services
- Semi-skilled trades
- Unskilled.

These broad category headings are not very illuminating. If you complete a census form, or for that matter any document which asks you to state what your occupation is, you often need to refer to an explanatory paragraph to give you guidance on what category you should choose. Without guidance, you could easily describe your occupation incorrectly. Take, for example, two categories from the above list:

1 *Security and protection services* A member of a police force or the armed services would obviously fit into this category. But would a police superintendent or a wing commander? It is perfectly legitimate to argue that both these ranks involve a large amount of managerial input on a day-to-day basis and should therefore be placed in the Managerial section. Which should take precedence?

2 *Professional* This definition is a minefield of interpretational problems. For example, if you are a doctor you are certainly in a profession, which undoubtedly makes you a professional. But equally you are someone who is involved in personal services when treating your patients. What happens if as part of your job with a Health Service Trust you are responsible for running a unit in a managerial capacity? Under all these circumstances, which occupational category do you belong to – Professional, Personal services or Managerial?

The above situations demonstrate the limitations of putting your occupation into descriptive categories which don't reflect the many *skills* you use during the course of your work. So, as a means of identifying your occupational skills, broad general categories are practically meaningless. Now look at the job description below:

Supervisor: You will be responsible for overseeing the work of a team of five and ensuring the team individually and collectively works efficiently and effectively. To achieve this you will be expected to have the following skills:

- good leadership and organisational abilities;
- excellent interpersonal and communication skills;
- the ability to act in a mentoring capacity.

All the above are qualities you would need to demonstrate in your role as a supervisor but they don't describe what abilities make *a good leader, a good organiser,* or *a good mentor.* These are quite separate skills, such as

- the ability to inspire confidence through example;
- the ability to evaluate information and take appropriate action;
- methodical work methods relevant to the task in hand;
- the ability to empathise with, counsel and guide others in an appropriate manner;
- good verbal communication pitched at different levels to meet different circumstances.

But this is still not the end of the story. This list only tells you what skills you have, not the *level* of ability you have in each skill.

Levels of ability

Your level of ability, or competence, in using a skill is as important as having the skill itself.

Your level of ability provides you with a means of assessing what you can do and what you can't.

Take the example of the supervisor again. The *number* of people you supervise is just as important. So although the *type* of skills you need to supervise one team or several teams is basically the same, the *level* of responsibility has risen, and so has the level of the individual skills needed to do the job successfully. For instance, you will need to:

◆ be competent in dealing with larger groups of people and the more complex interrelationships this involves;

◆ adapt and extend your work methods to show you are capable of supervising more than one team;

◆ be confident enough to talk to a larger group of people in a variety of settings, perhaps at formal and informal levels.

Off the top of your head, try to answer the following:

Thinking Slot 4

Have your previous jobs required

◆ similar skills?

◆ different skills?

◆ similar skills at different levels?

◆ different skills at different levels?

Skills in the home

> Home-based skills are probably the most overlooked and undervalued skills we have.

This shows up time and again when people want to return to work after taking a career break. Some have been bringing up children, others have been looking after elderly relatives for many years. The majority of people affected are women. They often feel that their long absence from the workplace puts them at a disadvantage. Their poor self-image is not helped by outdated attitudes that their skills are low-grade, low-key and not worth considering.

In Chapter 4 we shall be looking in depth at the range of skills to be found in the home and the extent to which they can be used as a bridge back into the paid working environment. But for the moment let's confine ourselves to thinking about these skills in a completely different way. Our starting point is once again the mundane task of shopping – not the leisurely pastime variety, but the necessary time-consuming business of buying essential supplies of food and other basic household goods.

Below is a list of the different stages of organising a shopping trip on your own. Next to this list, in brackets, is the equivalent activity in a paid employment context.

1   identifying items needed   (stock taking)
2   drawing up a list   (goal setting)
3   pricing items   (budgeting)
4   identifying outlets   (researching the market)
5   selecting alternatives   (strategy and decision-making)
6   paying for purchases   (financial management)
7   setting aside sufficient   (time management)
    time to complete the task

This is quite an impressive list of skills, however basic their level in this case. However, if the shopping expedition is extended to include someone else, or several people, an additional set of skills appears. For example:

8   agreeing who does what   (team working)
9   dividing up the list   (delegating)
10 splitting available funds   (budgetary control)
11 checking purchases   (monitoring and reviewing)

No one would pretend that because you are a successful shopper – you arrive home within the time you set yourself with all the items on your list having spent no more than you intended – then you are immediately capable of stepping into a high-level management job. What is important is that your successful shopping trip demonstrates you have management skills at a basic level.

Below is another opportunity to start thinking about home-based skills in a different light:

Thinking Slot 5

♦   What skills do you think are needed to be good at
    (a)   parenting?
    (b)   caring for the elderly?
    (c)   household budgeting?
    (d)   maintaining the home/garden/car?
    (e)   operating equipment in the home?
♦   How could you prove you had these skills?

Pastime skills

Skills linked to your spare-time activities are invaluable as signposts to the right sort of job to match your motivation and, just as important, the right sort of environment to match your personality.

In Chapter 5 we will be looking in greater detail at what you can discover about yourself from your spare-time interests. For the moment it is enough to start by dividing these interests into three groups:

1   Hobbies
2   Leisure pursuits
3   Voluntary work.

The reason for not lumping all these activities together under one heading is because separating them makes it easier to think about the very different motivational drives and different skills they each involve.

Hobbies

Hobbies can be thought of as activities: they are pastimes in which the stimulus comes from within yourself. You are motivated to *do* something. You play football or write fiction; you enjoy rambling or collecting stamps; you find being an amateur actor or painting in watercolours stimulating. With hobbies, you are actively involved and your involvement demands specialist knowledge or, at the very least, basic skills.

Leisure pursuits

Leisure pursuits are precisely that: the pursuit of leisure. Your involvement in them is largely passive: you are relying on someone else to provide the stimulus. You are a football supporter or avid reader; you watch TV or socialise at the pub; you go to the theatre, the art gallery or the cinema. To do any of these things you need no specialised knowledge to enjoy the experience: you are predominantly a spectator.

Voluntary work

Voluntary work, like having a hobby, is an active pastime. But in this case the benefits are not directly for yourself, but for others. You may, and probably do get indirect satisfaction from the service you provide, but this is only because you have given someone else pleasure or helped to make their life a little easier.

When we look at voluntary work in detail (Chapter 5), we will be looking at two distinct types: involvement with a national, regional or even local organisation, such as the Red Cross or your children's parents' association at school; and any personal commitments you may have which are not part of a formal group, such as regular shopping for an elderly neighbour or providing transport to and from hospital for someone outside your family.

Begin to think about your spare-time interests and answer the following:

Thinking Slot 6
- What sort of spare-time interests do you have?
  - hobbies?
  - leisure pursuits?
  - voluntary work?
- Are there other spare-time interests you would like to have?
- Which category do these belong to?
- Are there more interests in one category than the other two or are they spread fairly evenly across all three?
- What do you think this might tell you about your skills?

Interpersonal or social skills

Very few of us have no contact with other people on a day-to-day basis. Those who are isolated may not choose to be, but circumstances such as having few or no relatives living close by, old age, poor health or lack of transport have forced the situation on them. Some people actively seek solitude and are genuinely happier when they are on their own. But at some point, contact with the outside world has to take place.

> Interpersonal skills are important because human beings are by nature social animals.

Interpersonal skills are not skills which should be taken for granted. How we get on with those around us can improve our lives or, at the other extreme, destroy them. This is true whether we are at work, at home or at play.

The following list comprises a selection of interpersonal skills:

- good face-to-face communication
- good communication over the phone
- clear and concise writing abilities
- negotiation skills
- the ability to listen
- respect for other people's opinions
- the ability to persuade
- the ability to explain
- the ability to encourage
- the ability to admit to being in the wrong.

By just skimming over the list you can see how important these positive interpersonal skills are in oiling the wheels of our lives, and how the lack of them, or using negative skills such as bullying or being arrogant, can lead to conflict to a greater or lesser extent. These positive skills will be explored further in Chapter 6.

By using the above list of positive interpersonal skills, try to answer the following:

Thinking Slot 7
- Looking back over a recent conversation or incident at home, work or play, what interpersonal skills did you use to achieve what you wanted?
- Could you have used them more effectively to achieve the same end?
- Could you have used others?

Portable skills

Going back to the analogy of a life raft we used in the Preface, portable skills, or transferable skills as they are sometimes called, provide us with the most reliable planks to keep us afloat.

> Portable skills are the crucial life skills we can adapt and shape regardless of where we are and what stage we have reached in our lives.

We have already met them in many guises; what we will be doing in Chapter 7 is exploring their potential and how to use them to good effect.

The extraordinary property of a portable skill is its ability to be transferred from one set of circumstances to another. Skills learnt at school or college can be transferred to operate in the world of work or play. Some skills can be moved from one job to another. Others can be adapted from hobbies or voluntary work to provide skills in employment. The basic level of skills used in running a home have already been shown to provide a sound grounding for skills in the workplace. The other side of this coin can reveal work skills which can be transferred into the home during career breaks or long spells of unemployment. And finally, all the skills you have accrued from your many and varied activities, whether at home or in employment, can be put to good use when the world of work is behind you.

Retirement is not a word which conjures up an image of vitality or *joie de vivre* but, by using skills you have, you can avoid the stereotypical 'retired' scenario which too often includes the negative emotions of a sense of loss, or worthlessness. This is not to diminish the sadness you may feel at the loss of regular contact with colleagues, but this can easily be put into the context of moving on from one job to another. There are always new people to meet and other possibilities to explore. Knowing you have the skills to break the mould gives you the confidence to try out new ideas, or old ideas put on the back burner because you couldn't find time for them earlier. The second half of your life has the potential to be the most rewarding and everyone owes it to themselves to make sure that it is.

With this in mind, tackle the following challenge.

Thinking Slot 8
- Describe yourself using as many of your skills as you can think of.

Summary

Chapter 1 introduced you to different categories of life skills.

◆ Suggestions were made as to how you might want to record your findings when you investigate these skills in more detail in later chapters.

◆ The idea of a Personal Resource Pack (PRP) was introduced and how much time you should set aside to explore your potential was considered.

◆ You were given guidance on how to recognise what constituted a skill.

◆ At intervals you were invited to stop and think about some aspect of a skill to encourage you to begin describing yourself in a different way.

◆ At all stages you were shown you possess many more life skills than you might have given yourself credit for at first.

CHAPTER 2

Reviewing Educational Skills

T his chapter is *not* about educational qualifications, it is about skills you acquired during your academic career.

If you talk to teachers and pupils you find the emphasis is very much concentrated around what subjects are being taken and what grades everyone has got, or hopes to get, in their examinations. Success is still measured in numbers of examinations passed and at what level. There is nothing intrinsically wrong with this: after all, schools are routinely expected to achieve this type of success. The same applies to further or higher education. League tables have become a part of our lives, and anyone who is a parent knows there is a fascination in spotting where your offspring's school or university is in the long lists which annually appear in the national and local press.

Schoolday experiences

Your own experiences of education may be recent or dimming with the passage of time. Not everyone is prepared to admit their schooldays were the happiest days of their life, either because they found learning difficult, or the environment didn't suit them. They might have suffered from bullying or had poor relationships with certain members of staff which hindered progress.

If things went wrong in your own case, memories of your time in the education system can be coloured and distorted in such a way that you want to blot them out completely. Even when experiences of our school years were good, there is a tendency to recall the subjects that were taught, and not much else. As a result, we forget or simply overlook some of our involvement in the peripheral activities which were part of school or college life: the drama group, the football team, the choir, the orchestra, and so on. Yet it is these activities which often provide valuable clues to skills you have used, built on, or allowed to lie dormant.

Your journey of exploration to find the life skills buried in your educational past starts here: they are the first set of planks in your life raft.

Remembering life at primary school

Work on your Personal Resource Pack begins at this point. Get out your A4 pad, pens and pencils or bring up your PRP file on screen, head up the page with the title 'Educational skills' and leave the rest of the page blank: you will be completing this at a later stage.

Your first task will be simply to record details of the primary school or schools you attended. You may think this is a very odd, or even unnecessary exercise as part of an investigation into skills. Not so.

You will remember in Chapter 1 it was emphasised how important it was to put everything down on paper. This 'everything' includes simple recording of places, people and events. The reason for doing this is because by recalling and recording your personal history in detail, you can built up a picture of a time and place you might have long since ceased to think about.

> From this revived memory comes the opportunity to rediscover the source of some of your present skills, and more importantly perhaps, the existence of others you have allowed to fall into disuse.

Worksheet 1 is a suggestion for you to make use of. Remember it is only a guideline; it is entirely up to you how you choose to record your entries.

But before you begin, clear your mind of any distractions which might prevent you from concentrating on your task and relax. Only when you feel confident you are in the right frame of mind should you start to fill in the details.

Worksheet 1: Primary education

Name and location of school(s)	From	To

Set out below is the first of your Memory Joggers. As you meet these in the course of the book, include them as part of your PRP together with your responses to them. Don't rush to answer the questions raised. Close your eyes if it helps. Give the images time to develop and expand. If you went to more than one primary school, you will need to repeat this process for each school you attended.

Memory Jogger 1

1   Picture if you can everything about the school: the building; the playground; the teachers; the other children:
   ◆ describe the building, its architectural style, age and size;
   ◆ describe the playground and playing fields (if relevant) and any games areas marked out in them;
   ◆ name any of the teachers if you can, together with a description and any event you associate with that person, whether this was good or bad;
   ◆ name any friends you had during your time there.

2   Remember your life as a young schoolchild and the experiences these memories conjure up for you:
   ◆ How did you feel about yourself?
   ◆ How did the teachers treat you?
   ◆ How did you get on with your classmates?
   ◆ Did you find learning easy or difficult?
   ◆ How did you cope with the discipline, or lack of it?
   ◆ What was the highlight of your school day?
   ◆ What did you dread most?
   ◆ List which subjects you enjoyed most.
   ◆ List all the organised activities you took part in, e.g. nativity plays, recorder group, badminton club, chess club, sports days, art exhibitions etc.
3   Write down any other relevant recollections which come as flashes from the past – those which you have not thought about for years, or which up to now had been completely forgotten.

Read through what you have written several times. Refresh your memory so that you can feel confident about coming back to this material at a later stage and working on it in greater detail if you need to. Remember, too, that if any additional memories strike you later after you have moved on to another section of your PRP, or even if you are in the bath, peeling the potatoes, or driving the dog to the vet's, make sure you record them as soon as possible afterwards so they don't get forgotten again.

Remembering life at secondary school

We are now going to repeat the same process for your secondary education, except that some of the questions you will need to consider in the Memory Jogger will be more specific. Once again we start with the simple recording of facts with the details of the school or schools you attended. You should also include in this section any college you attended from the ages of 16–18 for the purposes of advanced level studies.

Worksheet 2: Secondary education

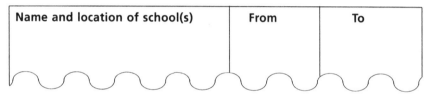

Name and location of school(s)	From	To

Next, because your Personal Resource Pack is also a work of reference, record details of the qualifications you gained.

Worksheet 3: School qualifications

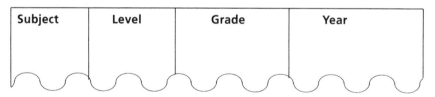

Subject	Level	Grade	Year

Now you have the facts at your fingertips, it's time for another Memory Jogger. Use the advice given on page 23 before you start to put you in the right frame of mind. And remember if you have any later thoughts on the topics covered, make sure you note these down. As before, complete the Memory Jogger for each separate secondary school, further education or sixth form college you attended.

Memory Jogger 2

1   Go through processes 1 and 2 set out in Memory Jogger 1 on page 24. Pay particular attention to the task of listing *all* the organised school clubs, societies, team activities you took part in, not forgetting the choir or orchestra.

2   List all the *informal* activities you took part in which the school didn't organise, but which were an accepted part of school life and took place on school premises, e.g. jazz or rock band; chamber music group; casual sports activities.

3   List all the *one-off* or *occasional* activities you were involved in, such as fund-raising events, production of a newsletter, plays, recitals, website construction etc.

4   List all positions of authority you held, such as prefect, head of house, team captain, event organiser, editor, director, lead violin etc.

5   List the three subjects you enjoyed most, with the names of the teachers. Think hard about this one – was it the *subject* you liked or the *teacher* who taught the subject? There is a difference. Did you take qualifications in these subjects and if not, why not? Would you like to study them again in the future?

6   Continue the thinking process as recommended in point 3 in Memory Jogger 1 on page 24.

Just as you were recommended to reread what you wrote down about your primary school days, you should do the same for the time you spent at secondary school, remembering too to add in anything which comes to you later which you hadn't included.

Remembering life at college or university

'College' for the purposes of this section should be taken to mean *any* educational institution you were enrolled in as an *adult*. this ensures that any educational achievements which may have come in fits and starts through your life, and not as a continuous process following on from school years, do not go unnoticed or unrecorded. This is particularly important for those who dropped away from their studies at some point, for whatever reason, but who later picked up where they left off and went on to achieve their goal.

This section should therefore include any full-time or part-time courses run by schools (other than the one you attended as a pupil), colleges of adult or further education, and correspondence institutes for the purposes of

(a) retaking school subjects to obtain higher grades;

(b) taking additional GCSEs/GNVQs; or

(c) taking additional Advanced GNVQs/AS Levels or A Levels.

The more obvious entries under this heading will be the degree courses run by universities (including the Open University) and further education colleges, as well as Higher National Diploma (HND) courses.

Professional qualifications which are *not* obtained through university degrees will be recorded in Chapter 3 when we look at occupational skills.

Record your college or university details as suggested in Worksheet 4.

Worksheet 4: College/university education

Name and location of college(s)	From	To

Once again, because your PRP is also a work of reference, record the courses you took and any qualifications you received on completion. The layout you choose in this case may need to be different from the one suggested in Worksheet 5 because of the many and varied course structures which exist, and you may want to devise a more personalised method of recording your achievements.

Worksheet 5: College/university qualifications

Course(s)	Subject(s)	Level of qualification

At this point, check you can find all your educational certificates, diplomas etc. and keep them in a safe place. You may feel it is now appropriate to combine them with your Personal Resource Pack.

Memory Jogger 3 which follows is slightly different from the two you have met so far. With so many course variations available it is not possible to devise one set of questions which would be universally useful to all college or university students. This is particularly so if you have had a string of part-time adult or further education courses over many years rather than full-time attendance at a university.

With this in mind, use the ideas in this Memory Jogger to meet your individual circumstances, skipping those parts which don't apply, particularly the first process which is designed to put in place a strong memory of time and place on which to build other memories. However, if you do feel there is a very strong memory associated with a part-time course, involving either the teacher/tutor or another student, and the circumstances were of some consequence to yourself, then this should be recorded.

Memory Jogger 3

1   Go through process 1 set out in Memory Jogger 1 on page 24 if this is relevant in your case.

2   Remembering the course:
 ◆ How did you feel about yourself?
 ◆ How did the tutors react to you?
 ◆ How did you get on with your peer group?
 ◆ Did you find the course easy or difficult?
 ◆ Did you get the qualification at the level you expected?
 ◆ Do you wish you had taken another course and if so, which one?
 ◆ List all the organisations and organised activities you took part in as a member of the student body, including the Students' Union, sports, arts, societies, groups etc.
 ◆ List any informal groups you were part of which could be loosely described as being part of college or university life, such as music and drama groups, campaigning groups etc.

3   Ensure you complete process 3 from Memory Jogger 1 on page 24.

Reviewing your Memory Joggers

It is useful at this stage to lay out your work on all three Memory Joggers in such a way that you can look quickly from one to another.

Starting with Memory Jogger 1 reread what you have written, pause for a while to absorb the material and then move on to 2 and 3 and repeat the process. In this way you will be able to refresh your memory, which is particularly important if you did not complete all three as a continuous process within a relatively short space of time.

If you have done a thorough piece of work on all three, you should have an excellent résumé of your reactions to your own very personal educational experiences. But you should also have something more:

- Clues about whether you grew in confidence as you got older or vice versa.
- Some idea about how teachers/tutors have reacted to you over the years and whether these reactions have changed over time.
- Whether the reaction of your peer group changed towards you over time.
- An indication of your approach to learning and whether this came easily when you were younger, or improved as your attitude and abilities matured.
- Whether there is a consistent interest in a particular subject or more general interest running through your educational history.
- Clues as to your preferences for different organised activities in formal surroundings and whether these changed with the passing years or not.

And finally:

- What significance there might be in your choice of informal group activities as an adult.

We will be looking again at this aspect in Chapter 5 when 'play' skills are explored further.

Look through your Joggers again using the ideas listed above. Jot down your thoughts and mull them over sufficiently so that you can draw some definite conclusions from them. If you are being honest with yourself in completing this task, not all your observations may be positive. You may, in fact, come to realise that you have been avoiding admitting there are negative facets in your life. You will have to be prepared for this. But *do* admit your mistakes or your shortcomings because by doing this you can take steps to repair the situation.

Thinking about your educational skills

Throughout this book there are going to be a series of skills audits relating to the topic covered by each chapter.

> The idea of the skills audit is to bring your abilities to the forefront of your attention.

Once you have done this, it becomes easier to focus on what abilities you have, or may have had in the past, and from that standpoint to focus on what you may be able to do with them both now and in the future.

For the remainder of this chapter we shall be concentrating not on your educational achievements themselves but on the skills you acquired while you were in the process of achieving them. We shall also be paying attention to the additional skills which came to light through your involvement in extra-curricular activities such as formal and informal clubs, societies, sports teams, drama, art and music groups, etc. And finally, we will be recognising the skills which emerged if you held any position of responsibility such as prefect, head of house, sports captain, lead violin, or the like.

To help you start this process we will begin by looking at the range of skills you are likely to have encountered to a greater or lesser extent during your time in a formal education environment.

The core skills

Under this heading we will be looking at literacy, numeracy and communication skills. As with all the skills audits in this book, the emphasis will be on *how can you prove you have these skills and to what level.* If you feel at any point that your skills in a particular area are not up to scratch, or what would be expected, have the courage to take this on board as a weakness which needs working on in future. Make a note of them on the self-assessment questionnaires you complete so you have no excuse for forgetting about them as you progress through the book.

Literacy skills

Literacy skills are reading and writing, and the important associated skill which comes from these – *comprehension*. Comprehension in this context is the process whereby we receive information in the *written* form and are asked to act on it, or provide a précis of it. Without comprehension we cannot understand instructions or rules or convey their meaning to anyone else.

Reading and writing skills should have been firmly established at primary school level. If they were not in your own case there may have been several reasons for this, e.g. long-term sickness or disruption caused by frequent moves. To be able to read and write effectively, you not only need to understand what words mean and have a vocabulary of around 2,000 words as a minimum requirement, you also have to have the ability to understand the structure of the language in which to place that vocabulary in a meaningful way. How confident are you in your literacy abilities?

Self-Assessment Questionnaire 1: Literacy skills

1   When were you competent at reading/writing/comprehension – primary school/secondary school/later?
2   If not at primary school, were there reasons for this and what were they?
3   How do you think you could demonstrate you are competent at each of these skills?
4   Do you believe you could improve these skills in any way and if so, how?

Numeracy

Numeracy, or at its simplest the ability to handle numbers through the processes of:

- adding
- subtracting
- multiplying and
- dividing,

is another of the core skills. Like literacy it is an essential skill in today's world where there are very few opportunities for paid employment without it. And like literacy, the basics of numeracy should have been in place by the time you left primary school.

Some people struggle with mathematics but don't find literacy skills difficult; others believe themselves to be poor at numeracy because they cannot deal with the more complex concepts of the subject at an advanced level. But not everyone needs to know how to calculate the effect of gravity to be able to hold down a demanding job or run a home. Where are you in the numeracy stakes?

Self-Assessment Questionnaire 2: Numeracy skills
1   How old were you when you stopped studying maths?
2   Do you think of yourself as being competent in basic maths, and if not, why not? Is this a true assessment of your abilities?
3   How would you go about demonstrating you were competent?
4   Do you feel you would like to improve your numeracy skills?

Speaking and listening skills

These two skills are also communication skills, the other side of the coin to the skills needed for written communication.

To be able to speak and listen effectively, you need a combination of foundation skills, such as the ability to speak and hear, and the ability to respond in a verbal, comprehensible form. As in literacy, you have to have a reasonably diverse vocabulary and the skill to weave the words together to convey meaning.

However, the written word and spoken word demand different abilities. An effective speaker uses a very different range of skills to that of the effective writer. The writer will tend to use longer sentences. The broadcaster or public speaker will keep it simpler or adapt the choice of words to match the occasion and the audience. The speaker can alter the tone of voice, pitch or speed of delivery, or use repetition to punch home a point. A single sentence can have a completely different meaning by emphasising a different word. For example take the simple sentence 'I am good'. In the way these three words are delivered there are three different meanings:

- *I* am good. (inferring someone else is not)
- I *am* good. (defending yourself against criticism)
- I am *good*. (adopting a high moral tone)

And the public speaker is even more effective if there is a clever use of body language skills and facial expressions to add emphasis.

The art of listening and speaking, in other words responding to what is being said to you, adds another layer of skills – the ability to assimilate what is being said, evaluate it and make a pertinent response immediately. These are the sort of skills you would need as a teacher, lawyer, politician or philosopher. At a much more mundane level, however, speaking and listening are part of the fabric of our everyday lives. Conversation and the interchange of ideas and information are taking place all the time – when we meet someone, go shopping in the high street or make a telephone call. How would you rate your verbal communications skills?

Self-Assessment Questionnaire 3: Speaking and listening skills

1 What occasions did you have at school/college to develop your verbal communication skills?
2 Are you confident in your ability to use them, and if not, why not?
3 Are you better communicating face-to-face or over the phone?
4 Are you able to get your point across in a public forum?
5 Do you feel you could improve the quality of your verbal communicating skills and in what way?

Computer literacy

Although not part of the three Rs, computer literacy or the ability to use the information technology which is all around us now, has become a core subject in the school curriculum. The impact of IT continues and looks increasingly likely to dominate our lives whether at work, rest or play.

IT is beginning to be a commonplace feature in the educational system. For many, it has played no part in their education at all. Today's children however are using computers for a range of educational activities, for example

- accessing databases for reference purposes;
- inputting data on to personal files for projects and coursework;
- designing graphics and electrical circuits;
- simple word processing.

Some schools and colleges have their own websites on the internet and pupils and students are encouraged to contribute to the design of these sites and the details put on them. It is becoming increasingly common for students to have school e-mail addresses.

Where are you with your IT skills?

Self-Assessment Questionnaire 4: IT skills

1 How much exposure have you had to IT skills as part of your education? Lots/some/not much/none.
2 If you have not gained these skills do you think you might need them in the future, and if so, which ones?
3 If you have IT skills, which ones are you using and are there others you think you would like to have?
4 How would you go about improving your IT skills?

Language skills

Under this heading we are looking at skills in languages other than English. These skills include reading, writing and speaking the language.

Most of us during our school years have had a brush with one foreign language or another, usually either French or German. Unless you have gone on to take a language course at a higher education level, the chances are that your competency in the language will be fairly low.

Taking on a foreign language is easier for some people if they learn it through conversation techniques which allow them to gain a reasonable level of fluency. Often under these circumstances, however, the grammar and structure of the language remain something of a mystery, and the written form a nightmare. Others master a language more readily off the printed page, but have difficulties coping with pronunciation and the rhythms of the verbal form. Those who are able to absorb a foreign language in all forms are very lucky indeed.

How you learn a foreign language therefore tells you something about the way you learn and the different skills these different ways of learning demand. Learning to speak the language through conversation demands a willingness to experiment, to make mistakes and to learn quickly through correction. Learning through studying the forms of the language demands a more step-by-step methodical approach, putting the grammatical structure in place before extending the vocabulary, with more emphasis on the written word rather than on the spoken.

How did you learn a foreign language?

Self-Assessment Questionnaire 5: Foreign language skills

1 What foreign languages did you study at school/college?
2 What level did you study to? Pre-GC(S)E/GC(S)E/A level/degree.
3 How would you describe your level of fluency? Good/middling/poor.
4 Which method(s) did you use to study?
5 Was this the right method for you and if not, do you believe you might have achieved more using alternative ways of learning?
6 Do you feel you would like to try to relearn a language or learn a new one?

Technical skills

Technology in today's educational terms has a variety of meanings: home economics (cooking and sewing to some of us); mechanical and electrical systems; design; graphic design and art.

Some of these subjects are taught in primary school, but the majority are studied at secondary school level.

There are two facets to these subjects which demand two very different sets of skills:

1 The ability to understand instructions and theories.
2 The ability to translate those instructions and theories into practical outcomes using tools, apparatus, equipment, instruments or computers.

These skills therefore are an interesting mix of the cerebral and the practical and one will not succeed without the other. There are so many skills involved in the individual subject areas, however, that it impractical to list them all here, but there are some basic skills which are common to all areas:

◆ literacy skills
◆ numeracy skills
◆ good hand/eye coordination.

Without these three basic skills, your technical skills are likely to be severely limited.

Self-Assessment Questionnaire 6: Technical skills
1   What technical subjects have you studied?
2   What skills did you need to succeed at these subjects?
3   Did you feel you lacked some skills which would have improved your level of performance?
4   Do you believe there might be some benefit in trying to improve these skills now?

Analysis and evaluation skills

These skills belong to secondary school years and beyond, where facts alone become only part of the educational process, and pupils and students are encouraged to question information and to form their own opinions based on their findings.

Analysis and evaluation skills are important life skills: they make us more aware of what is being said and done in the world around us, and provide us with the ability to make our own judgements. Almost without knowing it, we apply them to many situations in our everyday lives, from listening to the sales pitch of the door-to-door salesman to the speeches of our politicians, from reading newspaper articles to watching TV programmes. Without these skills we fall easy prey to the unscrupulous, the hypocrite and the con-artist.

To analyse and evaluate anything successfully you need to be able to work methodically through a series of processes, such as:

◆   collecting all the data necessary;
◆   recording this data correctly;
◆   examining the data in detail;
◆   coming to a conclusion;
◆   questioning the conclusion;
◆   confirming or refuting the conclusion; and in some cases
◆   reporting on these conclusions to others.

There are variations on this process depending on whether the analysis and evaluation has a definite outcome or is part of a continuous loop of review and monitoring.

Self-Assessment Questionnaire 7: Analysis and evaluation skills

1 What subjects did you study which helped develop your analysis and evaluation techniques?
2 Were you good at these subjects?
3 What evidence could you provide to show you have these skills?
4 Do you think this is an area of life skills you could develop further?

Time management skills

Very much one of the essential skills of the workplace, time management skills begin at school, particularly at the start of secondary school where homework and school examinations start to play a bigger part in our lives.

> In a time-dominated society, if you can't manage your time well, you've got a major problem.

Nothing will go right. You will get up late; miss your train or appointment; leave jobs unfinished, exam papers incomplete; be in a permanent muddle and have little or no control over your life.

To manage time well you have to be

◆ methodical in what you do;
◆ able to set priorities *correctly.*

Some of us will never make the grade because we are scatterbrained and disorganised by nature, while others of us are so organised we drive those around us to distraction.

Self-Assessment Questionnaire 8: Time management skills

1 Did you always submit your homework on time, and if not, why not?
2 Did you always, or mostly always, complete your examinations within the set timescale?
3 Do you find organising your day easy or difficult?
4 If you find it difficult is this because of the way you set about completing tasks, or because other people interrupt your progress?

5 Is time management a skill you feel you should, or could develop?

6 If so, how do you think you could achieve your goal?

Leadership skills

Job advertisements often include the need for leadership skills. For anyone who has been out of the job market for a while, or who has not held a position which demanded these skills, it is easy to forget that the foundations for these skills are often embedded in our schooldays.

What makes a good leader can depend on whether the group you are leading is formal or informal.

In formal situations at school, it is likely you were elected or appointed either by the teachers, or your peer group under teacher supervision, to be captain of a school sports team, a prefect, head girl or boy, head of house, editor of the school magazine, club or society organiser, the person in charge of charity fund-raising etc. Unless there was some unexpected event, you were likely to hold this position for a specific length of time.

In informal situations generally, where the group is a social entity rather than part of a structured organisation, leadership evolves from common consent that one of the group should take the leading or dominant role in decision-making. In these circumstances, the group may decide to change its leader as often as it feels the need.

Most of us have experienced informal groups at school, either as a result of mixing with classmates taking the same subjects as ourselves, or by belonging to the same form or year group. It was possible to belong to several different groups at the same time if the school operated a 'streaming' or 'set' system for different subjects.

Good leadership is about having the ability to command authority through:

- taking the lead;
- showing excellence by example;
- encouraging others;
- delegating roles to others;
- advising, counselling and guiding others;
- accepting criticism in a positive way;

◆ relating positively to others;
◆ taking responsibility for both one's own actions and those of the group.

You also need to be in possession of good listening and speaking communication skills to be effective in the role.

Self-Assessment Questionnaire 9: Leadership skills

1　What leadership roles did you have at school/college?
2　How could you prove you were successful in these roles?
3　How do you think you might have improved your leadership qualities?
4　Would you have liked to be a leader but were never given the chance?
5　What do you believe stopped you from being chosen?
6　What skills do you need to develop if you want leadership roles again?

Working as one of a team

Team skills are very much in demand in the workplace. They include leadership, but extend to other abilities which are needed to make a team work successfully to achieve its goal. To be effective a team needs a range of individuals with different skills.

The obvious team at school or college is the sports team where the position you hold in the field or on the court tells you what your role should be – defence or attack. But there are other teams within the school/college context at a formal and informal level which should not be forgotten and where roles are defined in a different way. For example, the orchestra, the choir, drama group, jazz group, rock band and so on. In these cases, the skills to play an instrument, act or sing are very different, but the skills needed to make the group effective remain the same.

To be a good teamworker you need the personal qualities of being able to:

◆ tolerate others' opinions;
◆ put forward your own views based on sound judgement;
◆ accept a majority decision;

- make the majority decision work;
- accept leadership and discipline.

Some teamworking involves additional skills, such as the ability to:

- initiate ideas for the team to use;
- reflect on ideas and evaluate their value;
- organise ideas into practical activities for the team;
- monitor the progress of activities;
- review the activities against the original intention.

You can see that not only are interpersonal and communication skills essential for good teamworking, but also analysis and evaluation skills, as well as creative thinking.

Self-Assessment Questionnaire 10: Teamworking skills

1   What team roles did you have at school or college?
2   Do you enjoy working as part of a team, or do you prefer working on your own?
3   What teamworking skills would you like to develop?
4   How do you think you could do this?

Skills from individual self-expression

These are the skills which belong to those who are creative, in the widest sense of the word: artists, designers, architects, craftsmen, writers, dancers, singers, musicians, actors, directors, composers, sculptors, chefs, landscape gardeners – the list is enormous.

We get our introduction to these skills even before we start school. In primary school they become more structured as part of our lessons or as end-of-term activities, such as the nativity play or junior orchestra concert. These young skills are taken with us into secondary school and on into college. Many of the skills are used for a while but are lost as pressures from other subjects or interests take over. You may feel your single excursion into the dramatic arts as the third shepherd at the age of eight when you had four lines to learn is not worth the trouble of remembering. But don't be tempted to ignore this personal triumph, because that is precisely what it is.

Self-expression is all about getting yourself across to a wider audience. How you do this will vary according to the discipline you are following. For the artist and designer it may be through the skilful draughtsmanship displayed in the finished product. For the actor, dancer or musician it may be the emotional quality they bring to a work.

The performing skills are the most valuable because what you make or do is taking place in front of an audience.

> Your ability to present yourself and play your part to perfection are exactly the same skills you need to bring to your role as an applicant at a job interview.

Which is why being the third shepherd at the age of eight should be looked on as an important event in your life.

Self-Assessment Questionnaire 11: Creative skills
1   Are your creative skills in the non-performing or performing category?
2   Which ones did you develop at school/college?
3   Are there any you have let slip and would like to revitalise?
4   Are there any new creative skills you would like to try?
5   What's stopping you doing them now?

Interpersonal skills

We have already mentioned in passing that some of the skills we have been looking at need some level of interpersonal skills input as well, e.g. leadership and teamworking, language and verbal communication skills. At any point in our lives where we have to interact with other people, we need to make that interaction a satisfactory experience.

Our basic interpersonal skills are learnt in the home well before we go to school. Here, among people we know, we learn we can't always get what we want from other people when we want it; that there needs to be give and take on all sides to maintain harmony in the household; that how we treat adults, our siblings and friends usually requires some fine turning to get the best results.

Once we go to school, we learn to refine our skills and adapt our way of approaching new relationships which demand we work and play with complete strangers. In this way we are prepared for the rest of our lives, and sometimes we find we don't master these skills too well. Interpersonal chemistry can sometimes produce an explosive mix when personalities collide, and this is usually in no one's best interest.

Good interpersonal skills are quite sophisticated: they demand a fair amount of mental agility to meet the unexpected, as well as the expected. These are communication skills in their highest form, so if you ever fancied being a diplomat, you need them in abundance. They involve the ability to:

- rapidly assimilate a situation, body language, tone of voice, expression and choice of language;
- adapt personal responses accordingly;
- use body language, tone of voice, expression and choice of language appropriate to meet the desired outcome of the encounter;
- use persuasive language effectively;
- negotiate to achieve an outcome acceptable to all.

Self-Assessment Questionnaire 12: Interpersonal skills

1   Were there any occasions at school/college when you felt you lacked good interpersonal skills?
2   Do you feel that by the end of your education you had improved these skills, and if so how had you improved them?
3   Are you aware of any shortcomings in your interpersonal skills, and if so, what are they?
4   Can you think of any ways you could improve these skills?

Once you have completed these questionnaires, file them in a section set aside for them in your Personal Resource Pack.

Tackling your educational skills audit

So far we have been digging into the past to encourage you to review your school and college years in a different way, and to start identifying some of the skills you acquired in the process of being educated.

The self-assessment questionnaires were the start of the audit process. The audit itself will need you to translate your personal educational history and experiences into a skills-based format using the skills we have been considering earlier.

Start the audit itself with Worksheet 6.

Worksheet 6: Skills from subjects studied for examination

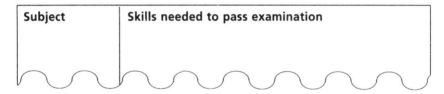

Subject	Skills needed to pass examination

List each subject you were examined in and next to it identify all those skills you needed to use in order to study the subject successfully. Incidentally, as mentioned earlier, in passing an examination it goes without saying that at least two of the skills you need to include in your list are:

◆ literacy
◆ time management.

Next, turn to Memory Joggers 1, 2 and 3. From these you need to extract details of all your activities, one-off events and the recognised positions you held. Enter all this information on Worksheet 7.

Worksheet 7: Activities at school/college/university

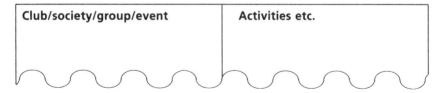

Club/society/group/event	Activities etc.

Break down the activities into separate elements. For example, if you were a member of the school hockey team say whether you were in the A team, B team, or whatever. Note down the position or positions you played in; whether the team was particularly noteworthy in its league; whether it won any of the competitions it took part in (and the dates, don't forget), and so on.

Next from your Memory Joggers make a list on Worksheet 8 of all the recognised positions you held either at school or college, and itemise separately the duties and responsibilities which went with the post. (If you were captain of a sports team you listed on Worksheet 7, you will need to make a separate entry here for the position of captain: the skills involved in both will be different and both need to be recorded.)

Worksheet 8: Positions held at school/college/university

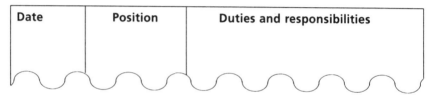

Date	Position	Duties and responsibilities

Next, transfer your list of activities onto separate Worksheets 9 and 10 (educational skills audits) as set out on page 45.

The suggested layout includes the sections, 'What I achieved' and 'Evidence of achievement'. 'What I achieved' allows you to record details of any personal success in that specific activity. 'Evidence of achievement' should include details of any prizes, cups, medals or certificates awarded as proof of the achievement or recognition of the standard reached. At this point you should also think about what other evidence you may have, or perhaps even your parents have, such as photographs, press cuttings, testimonials or letters of appreciation, which support your case. It is a good idea to collect these into a scrapbook or scrapbook format to be amalgamated into your Personal Resource Pack. These items often get discarded as not being particularly relevant as time goes on and your interests or lifestyle change. If you have not been keeping them in the past, it is a good idea to start now. They are not only helpful as part of the process of reminding you of your successes, they act as a morale booster in their own right when life is less than rosy.

Remember to adapt the suggested layout to meet your own requirements. Don't stint your entries just because it means going over onto another page. Skills come in all shapes and sizes, so you may find it useful to reread the section 'Recognising your skills and abilities' on page 5 at this stage.

Finally, extract all the skills you have recorded on Worksheets 7, 9 and 10 and print them in a simple list format under your original heading 'Educational skills' which you left blank at the start of this chapter. Put this list at the front of your educational Worksheets in your PRP.

Worksheet 9: Educational skills audit: Skills from school/college/university activities

Activity

Date (or length of involvement):

The skills I used were:

What I achieved:

Evidence of achievement:

Worksheet 10: Educational skills audit: Skills from positions held at school/college/university

Position held

Date (or length of involvement):

The skills I used were:

What I achieved:

Evidence of achievement:

Summary

Chapter 2 has concentrated on the life skills you may have acquired from your educational experiences.

- You were encouraged through the use of Memory Joggers to remember aspects of your life at the different schools and colleges.
- You were asked to make a record of your academic qualifications for your Personal Resource Pack.
- You were asked to identify the range of skills you used during your academic career.
- By completing Self-Assessment Questionnaires you began to identify occasions when you used these skills and how they related to situations later in life.
- By using these and your Memory Joggers you then went on to complete your educational skills audit.

Give us the
tools, and we
will finish the
job.
SIR WINSTON
CHURCHILL

CHAPTER 3

Investigating Occupational Skills

Governments in recent years have been concerned with the lack of skills available in the workforce to meet the perceived needs of the new century. There has been a flurry of activity around the concept of lifelong learning and the encouragement of people not to put the idea of learning behind them once they have gone into employment.

The introduction of skills-based National Vocational Qualifications (NVQs) as recognised awards for on-the-job training have allowed many employees the opportunity to gain qualifications on a part-time basis. Businesses too have been encouraged to seek recognition of their commitment to employee training through the Investors in People (IIP) awards.

Learning for life

But lifelong learning is not just about learning for work, it is about learning for life. Once you have the skills to achieve in one area, you have the foundation stones for adapting those skills for other purposes.

> The skills you acquire in the workplace are just as transferable as any others: you carry them with you, from job to job, from job to hobbies, from hobbies to home, from home to job.

Before you can feel confident in taking on any new venture, you need to satisfy yourself you have the abilities to make a success of it. In this chapter we will be looking at your employment record to date, the sorts of jobs you have been employed in, and the types of skills you were using to carry out your duties efficiently. These skills are the second set of planks for your life raft.

To do this we need to start by making a record for your Personal Resource Pack of any professional or occupational qualifications you hold, and your employment record to date. But before you do anything else, open up a new file entitled 'Occupational skills' and leave the rest of the page blank to complete later. If you have no entries to put into either of these categories then skip this section and go on to page 49 where we start looking at the range and type of skills which are needed in the workplace.

Professional or occupational qualifications

The reason for recording your professional or occupational qualifications here rather than in Chapter 2 is because it is better if these work-related qualifications are clearly identified within your PRP as part of your occupational history.

When you record the basic facts of any occupational qualifications gained, allow yourself sufficient space in your record to list the subjects that were part of the course. This is particularly important if you have completed a qualification which covers several areas of study with optional modules. Over the passage of time it is easy to forget these, but individually they may count towards accreditation for future courses, or show that you have a level of understanding of a subject which might be rekindled in a different way later in life, or even provide the foundation for future training in other fields.

As with your educational certificates, make sure you know where your occupational qualifications are in case you need to produce them for reference purposes, either for future employment or as support documents when applying for credit transfer claims for other courses of study. You may prefer to keep them with your Personal Resource Pack.

A suggested layout to record your occupational qualifications is set out in Worksheet 11 (page 48). If you feel it would be useful to include other details, such as how you studied (full-time, part-time, distance learning etc.) and notes on any projects which formed part of the course and what these involved, then do so. How you learned tells you something about your learning skills and their strengths and weaknesses. The successful completion of project work demands the skills of time management and self-motivation, both of which are useful work skills in themselves.

Worksheet 11: Professional/occupational qualifications gained

Awarding body	Date	Qualification	Subjects studied

Recording your work history

Make Worksheet 12 a simple, straightforward record of all your jobs to date *including any casual, part-time or temporary employment of a short duration.* This type of employment would not usually play much of a part in your employment record, particularly if you've had a string of short-term jobs which you might have lumped together to prevent an awkward gap in your application form, or given them little more than a one-line mention.

For the purposes of your skills audit, however, *all* your paid work experiences count.

> There may be something about one of those casual, short-term jobs which particularly appealed to you, and might possibly appeal to you again in the future.

Remember your promise to yourself – **don't discount anything.**

When you complete the details under 'Duties and responsibilities' try to reduce these to a series of one-line statements. If you do this, it will be easier for you later to look at each of these statements in turn and break them down into a series of descriptive action terms using the *-ing* skills words (see page 5).

Worksheet 12: Employment history

Employer and job title	From	To	Duties and responsibilities

Putting yourself into a workstyle category

Up until the mid-1990s, jobs could be put into four simple categories which described their main functions:

- Thinking
- Organising
- Administering
- Doing.

These are all broad descriptive terms for the skills needed to do the job well.

Thinking skills

These skills are essential in such jobs as research and development, policy-making, designing and the like where the main thrust of the job is generating ideas, strategies or drawing up policies.

Organising skills

These are skills which involve putting ideas, strategies or policies into a structured format to produce a coherent framework for operational activities.

Administering skills

These skills involve the smooth running and monitoring of the operational activities to achieve the desired outcome of the ideas, strategies or policies.

Doing skills

These are all the skills necessary to complete the operational activities which are essential to bring the ideas, strategies and policies into fruition.

Since the mid-1990s, however, the introduction of computer technology into practically every workplace has blurred the edges of these comfortably broad categories. Thinkers using dedicated computer software can at the click of a mouse test their theories on screen and become Doers; Organisers using spreadsheets can administer their own systems; Administrators can revise structures to meet changing demands, and Doers can generate their own feedback and monitoring by inputting relevant data.

What this means *in terms of employment skills* is that almost without exception there is now a general understanding that such skills will include computer literacy of one sort or another. There are very few jobs indeed available in this new century which remain untouched by the computer to some degree, and those which are tend to be either purely creative, or in the service sector at the lower end of the pay scale, e.g. in catering, in small retail outlets and waste disposal.

Looking at different spheres of work

Workstyle categories are one way of looking at your skills. There is another. If you think of your jobs as being plotted on a graph, workstyle categories occupy one axis, and on the other are the different spheres of work.

It is possible to divide work into four spheres of activity and most employment involves at least two of them. Put simply these spheres can be described as:

- dealing with people or animals
- manufacturing products
- managing finance
- involving creativity.

Each of these spheres has its own range of skills and in the following sections we will be looking at each sphere in turn and investigating some of the skills needed for each. You will notice there that each skill is described by an *-ing* word.

Dealing with people or animals

These are the sort of skills you need for *any* job where you have contact with the public or responsibility for the well-being or safety of people or animals.

These skills are needed not just in those jobs in the caring sector which immediately spring to mind, such as doctors, nurses, veterinary surgeons, teachers and social worker, as well as the numerous ancillary jobs to these professions. There are many other jobs, both professional and otherwise, where contact with the public or animals is either wholly or partially involved. Take, for instance, taxi drivers, airline pilots, sales assistants, riding instructors or dog breeders – a wide diversity of roles where people or animals are dependent on their skills.

Carrying out orders or instructions

This will usually require at least basic literacy skills, together with the supplementary skills associated with the necessary knowledge or experience, e.g. safety, first aid or evacuation procedures; timetable schedules; landing instructions or meat inspection directives.

Maintaining/caring

Maintenance and caring roles by non-professionals may nonetheless include an elementary level of professional skills, such as the administration of medicines or the regular checking of temperatures. But they can also include other functions such as monitoring food intake, food preparation, washing or grooming, cleaning and other personal services. These require skills in food, personal and animal hygiene; dietary and nutritional knowledge; hair/fur and skin care, pedicure and so on.

Of paramount importance in all these jobs, however, is a good level of interpersonal skills and the ability to inspire confidence, combined very often with genuine understanding and a sympathetic approach.

Serving

These skills are part of any job where you are not in a position of recognised status or authority as far as your clientele is concerned. Knowing how to deal with customers, clients or any member of the public demands a high level of interpersonal skills, and in many cases a great deal of personal self-control.

As a society, we seem to be getting ruder and more violent in our reactions to others and to situations we disagree with, as increasing incidents of assaults on health workers, other road users and air passengers illustrate.

> The avoidance of conflict through a mixture of negotiation skills and body language techniques is now almost a prerequisite for anyone in the service industries.

And, of course, good verbal communication skills are a must for anyone dealing with the public over the phone.

Communicating

Communication skills have already been touched on in connection with serving. However, good communication skills are crucial when you are employed in any role where you not only have to listen or read accurately, but also have to make a clearly understandable response. In these situations waffle may not only confuse but has the potential to be downright dangerous. Air traffic controllers, driving instructors and chemistry teachers are just three examples of jobs where incoherent, imprecise or inaccurate information could prove fatal.

But there are other sorts of communication skills which are not about the carefully chosen word itself but about the way in which the word is broadcast. In this category are the sign languages used by deaf people, semaphore and the now defunct Morse code. The skills associated with these types of communication involve the assimilation of completely different *methods* of communicating a 'language', including being able to understand the complexities of 'grammar' and 'syntax' within the context of the language being used.

There are also the complex skills associated with using Braille, where communication is constrained by the ability to convey meaning through a series of raised dots on a page and to translate these through touch into a meaningful sentence. Taking notes in shorthand and transcribing them demands the ability to think and write very precisely in symbols – a skill shared with the mathematician setting down a formula to convey a theory, law or hypothesis. In these skills there is no room for error.

Persuading

Persuading people means you have to be competent in either written or oral communication. Sub-skills in this category include encouraging and negotiating, which form part of the job of anyone who has to offer advice and guidance. It is an essential skill for people who work in industrial relations, the law, medicine, teaching or the armed forces and also covers jobs in the areas of selling or purchasing. Selling can include the sale of products, services or ideas, and covers a wide range of occupations such as salesman, financial adviser or politician.

There obviously has to be a heavy emphasis on interpersonal skills if you want to be able to influence people's opinions or actions, or to convince them to part with their money.

Recording

Where you are in paid employment helping people or animals, you will be expected to be able to record details of those you help. Bureaucracy and legislation demand more and more records: personal details and background; addresses; services offered, given or refused; medical history; daily activities; dietary requirements; accident reports and so on.

Apart from the basic ability to write, you may also need to be able to maintain records. This can include initiating the original record, inputting regular updates, editing, sorting and ultimately disposing, erasing or storing the record according to procedural instructions. All these actions require evaluation skills if your record keeping is to be efficient and effective.

Advising

Anyone directly in charge of people (rather than just caring for them) must have this ability. This skill sometimes includes the associated abilities of training, monitoring and supervising under circumstances where a 'light touch' is needed to get the right response, and where the recipient could choose not to follow the advice offered. A high level of interpersonal and persuasive skills is essential to produce a successful outcome. Health professionals, business advisers and social workers come within this field.

Instructing

These skills are closely linked to advisory skills, but with one important difference, the role involved is one of authority. In this situation there is the element of compulsion and the expectation that the person or animal will comply with any orders or instructions given. The interpersonal skills essential to be successful are the same as for advisory roles but with the additional ability to obtain compliance either through leadership skills or by virtue of the position and its perceived status. (If you are in a position of authority, you ought to be in possession of leadership skills, but this does not necessarily hold true.)

Associated skills include delegating, organising and coordinating, usually in connection with subordinates who may

also be in authority over others. This is particularly true of the
police, prison, probation or armed services, but may also apply
within hospital and teaching environments.

Manufacturing products

Because manufacturing covers such a wide range of products, the
skills being discussed here have to be broad-brush headings only.
Under them, a whole series of specific skills would have to be
listed according to the type of work being done.

Following procedures

No product can be manufactured without a procedure of one sort
or another being followed in strict sequencing: A plus B making
C, where B plus A would produce the wrong result or no result at
all. You cannot manufacture a car or assemble furniture if you put
the pieces together in the wrong order. The ability to follow
procedures which are written down or which are picked up by
watching how it is done are both important skills in the
production process, but they are different: basic literacy is
required on one hand, and the ability to assimilate information
through observation on the other.

Handling and manipulating

The skills needed to handle goods being produced can involve the
extremes from managing heavy machinery and tools associated
with traditional industries to the delicacy of touch needed in the
manufacture of microchips. Both of these and all the shades
between demand good hand-to-eye coordination and other
physical skills.

Operating

This skill is usually associated with machine minding. It requires a
knowledge of the workings of the machine and the ability to use it
and monitor its performance to ensure production takes place. A
machine minder may also need the skills to set up, repair or
adjust the machine in the event of a fault occurring and to be
able to devise test runs to ensure its proper functioning
afterwards.

Driving

Fork lift trucks, loaders, stackers, lorries, HGVs delivering raw
materials and taking away finished products are all part of the

manufacturing scene. Driving a car is a skill which is so easily overlooked because it is now so commonplace, while driving any other vehicle demands different skills again to meet the function of the vehicle.

Controlling and monitoring

Similar to operating, these skills are more to do with how processes occur and how much direction of the process has to be input by the operative in charge. In this type of situation, the operative, unlike the machine minder, is unlikely to be able to leave the process unattended. Controlling is all about constant vigilance, adjustment and readjustment, testing and retesting, and evaluation.

Measuring

Measuring can involve several things. For instance, the physical act of weighing out quantities, supervising the use of specific quantities of raw materials in the production process, or watching pressure gauges, temperature readings or the like. Good hand-eye coordination is needed in the first example, the ability to monitor the different processes applies in the case of the other two.

Recording

Recording for the purpose of product manufacturing can be spread across the whole range of processes involved, starting with booking in the raw materials into the warehouse; noting the volumes used during the course of manufacturing; detailing the number of units made, spoiled or discarded for quality control purposes; registering items placed in the warehouse ready for distribution, and finally checking off items as they leave the warehouse for sale.

Recording skills always demand attention to detail whether people, animals or products are involved.

Managing finance

The skills under this heading are not just those you would expect to see within a recognised financial institution such as a bank or building society. Managing finance in this context is meant to encompass that part of a business or organisation which handles finance, whether this is cash or credit for goods or services received, or drawing up budgets and financial strategies. Financial management does not always demand high level numeracy skills in areas which are more to do with policy or regulation, but elsewhere numeracy skills are essential, although they may be specialised and devoted to the practical running of a business, not those demanded of a theorist or engineer.

Applying rules

Financial management is very heavily regulated by legal requirements and regulations. These are imposed both externally by central government, the Inland Revenue and watchdog bodies to ensure probity and reduce tax avoidance, and internally by procedures imposed to reduce fraud, mismanagement of funds and to satisfy audit inspections.

Financial managers have to be able to understand the complexities of what is required by the various rules and to be able to put the requirements into practice to comply with them. The phraseology used often demands more than a simple level of basic literacy to understand what is required, combined with additional skills depending on the level of work and the type of job being undertaken.

Accounting and maintaining financial records

Accountancy demands a rigorous process of recording financial transactions from which a business can work out whether its trading position is viable or otherwise. It is more than book-keeping, although book-keeping is part of the process, and at the top level it requires the input of a qualified accountant who has satisfactorily completed a course of training in accountancy skills.

Maintaining financial records, however, can be the responsibility of a quite lowly employee. A shop assistant completing a takings sheet at the end of a day and responsible for banking monies received is maintaining a financial record, so is the petrol pump attendant who notes down the amount of petrol to be invoiced to a business customer. It goes without saying that basic numeracy skills are essential, but so is attention to detail in transferring figures from one format to another.

Monitoring

Financial monitoring involves regularly reviewing the activities of a business or organisation to check that it is operating within its budget and if it is not, why this has occurred, and what needs to be done to rectify the situation. Monitoring usually takes place as part of a management function and needs the skill of translating facts and figures into an accurate picture of the state of the business, as well as being able to spot a flaw in the numerical statements for unofficial or official audit purposes.

Budgeting and assessing

Budgeting is the skill of using figures for the previous year's income and expenditure as a base line and, by taking into account the fixed and possible variable factors of that particular business or organisation, setting limits on the costs the business can afford during the year to come. It is not the skill of crystal-ball gazing, but an honest attempt to put together a financial framework around which the business can operate successfully, think about expanding, or face cutbacks and possible closure.

Assessing costs is part of the budgeting process and needs experience or knowledge of likely costs and confidence about the basis on which any estimate is made. You need to be able to make judgements about the potential financial demands on all aspects of a business or organisation and be able to justify your figures if necessary.

Allocating and granting funds

If you are responsible for allocating and granting funds you are likely to be bound by rules and procedures under which monies can be given or loaned. There may or may not be some flexibility in how you interpret the rules or procedures; there may also be certain criteria which have to be met before you can consider any request. To function effectively you need to be skilled in applying these criteria and interpreting any guidance or directive which governs them.

Calculating

Calculating correctly is of paramount importance whether it involves the total cost of purchases made by a customer in your shop, or setting the index of average earnings in the Office of National Statistics. Incorrect calculations can lose a business money or see an unnecessary increase in interest rates which can adversely affect the whole economy. The skills needed are just as diverse, comprising basic numeracy on the one hand, to enumeration based on a variety of inputs and statistical information on the other.

Working creatively

There is a tendency to think about creativity as being the preserve of the arts, whether this is writing, painting, sculpture, music, drama or dance. Creativity, however, not limited to such a narrow interpretation: it is a range of skills which includes not just the broad spectrum of the arts, but also takes in the inventiveness of the sciences, and the innovative approach to producing ideas and tackling problems found in many organisational settings.

It may be very prosaic, such as devising a new form to be completed by job applicants, but it is now well recognised that the way forms are designed can have considerable impact on the quality of the information they provide – which is why so much effort is put into devising not just the questions, but also how the forms should be laid out to encourage a positive response.

> Organisations cannot survive without some creative input.

Companies large and small use advertisements, either to sell their goods and services, or to sell themselves as being 'eco-friendly', 'caring' etc. Some of the best quality TV can be found in the creativity and inventiveness of many of the advertisements which have become art-forms in themselves.

Brainstorming

An ability to brainstorm, i.e. to let your mind freewheel and come up with a whole range of ideas from the whacky to the brilliant, is part of the process of thinking through ideas and problem-solving in a creative way. It is sometimes linked to the ability to think laterally, a way of approaching and tackling problems from a completely different perspective which does not follow the usual run-of-the-mill thought processes. Brainstorming itself does not necessarily involve evaluating the ideas put forward: the emphasis is much more on the generation of ideas which others can test for validity.

Devising solutions

This is the other side of the coin to brainstorming: the more analytical, step-by-step approach to resolving a problem. It is likely to involve the ability to evaluate the ideas put forward in a critical manner, test the hypotheses and build on the findings. It is therefore a much more incremental approach which stops only when a solution is found. This type of problem-solving is much more likely in a research and development environment but applies equally in such diverse scenarios as aircraft or car design, criminal investigations, engineering projects or code-breaking.

Creating or composing

Creating in this sense is limited to abilities in the artistic sphere. This may involve a personal skill where as an individual you are responsible for an outcome, whether this is a painting, a tapestry, a novel or play, a sculpture, a symphony or any other piece of work which could come under the collective umbrella of 'a work of art'. Equally, the outcome might be a collective production, the amalgamation of several skills of which yours is a part of the whole. The most obvious examples of this are acting in or directing a film or play, but can equally be applied to any group of skilled people working towards a defined goal, e.g. seamstresses for a fashion house.

Composing may be an individual musical skill or a collaboration with others who have the same or complementary skills. These can be instrumental or vocal abilities. Linked into skills associated with music are those of choreography which has crossed over from the world of dance into gymnastics, ice skating and even swimming. The skills of choreography depend largely on knowledge of the medium being choreographed and the demands it makes on performers.

Manipulating or handling

These skills run across the board from art to science and are the basic physical skills of good coordination and manual dexterity. They apply whether you are in a science laboratory making minute adjustments to experimental procedures or playing the lead violin in a symphony orchestra.

However, it is possible for those who have lost the use of their hands to create works of art by holding their drawing materials between their teeth or their toes, and the advances in computer technology have provided numerous alternatives to dexterity for those with extremes of disability. There are therefore far more openings now for the disabled to demonstrate their skills in both the arts and sciences than there were even a decade ago. Stephen Hawking is a shining example in the field of science.

Performing and interpreting

On the artistic side, performing is your personal interpretation of how a piece of music should be played; how a character in a play or ballet should be portrayed; how a song should be sung. Others may direct or advise you, but ultimately, how you perform is dependent on you. The performance itself may be in public, in a studio or on a film set; you may be a soloist or part of an ensemble; there may be technical gadgetry to cope with. To be a good performer you have to be able to contend with anything and everything – and prove you can. The show, as they say, must go on.

But what might be called 'the performing arts' are not limited to the world of the artist. To be able to speak clearly and confidently in public is a skill in itself, and many people find it daunting. Most of us at some time or other have experienced a formal interview.

Interpreting what is expected of us is a social skill. We adapt our language and often our dress to suit the occasion; we weigh up other people's reactions to us and adjust our responses accordingly; we learn when it is appropriate to act or speak, and when it would be counterproductive. In these situations, we are moulding the skills of the performer to help us in our social exchanges.

> The supporting skills associated with acting, i.e. vocal presentation, body language, adopting a role, are enormously helpful in any interview situation.

Creating new entities

Creativity, as already stressed, is not just the preserve of the artist. In the business world the entrepreneur creates new ventures; politicians create new parties; inventors create new concepts. Each of these spheres of activity involves completely different environments, but the fundamental spark which makes creativity what it is remains the same. Any activity which involves producing, devising, structuring something which was not in existence before has this grain in it.

Tackling your occupational skills audit

It's now time to move on from simply thinking about what sort of skills can be found in the workplace to starting the process of identifying your own.

There is nothing prescriptive about what is being recommended here and it remains your own choice as to how much or how little you explore the possibilities open to you. Having said this, however, it is obvious that if you want your explorations to be of some use to you then you need to investigate the skills you employed in more than one job or, if the case applies, more than one sphere of work.

Perhaps the best guiding factor in your choice of which jobs you want to look at in greater detail, is what you would like to find out most from your investigations. You may be simply curious about the range of skills you have been using in the last five or ten years; or you may be more interested in seeing if the *level* of skills you have been using in several jobs in the same sphere of work has been increasing year on year or has reached a plateau. You may even think it is worthwhile going through the process with every single job on your list if you are facing a crisis in your life or reaching a turning point. Knowing what you can do and how well you can do it is probably one of the best ways of helping yourself to make and take decisions.

Once you have chosen your preferred method of working, go back to your employment history (Worksheet 12) and the list of one-line statements you made under the heading 'Duties and responsibilities'. The next stage is to take each of these statements in turn and break them down into a series of skills needed to do the job effectively. This should be done using Worksheet 13 as set out on page 63. It isn't necessary to go into detail about the intricacies of the job, just the skills you used. For example, if you were a contact person for a helpline, your one-line statements under 'Duties and responsibilities' might include:

- Taking initial contact calls from members of the public.
- Answering queries within my remit.
- Referring other queries to relevant section.

Looking at the first responsibility, the skills involved would be along the following lines:

- Listening to the query.
- Identifying the problem.
- Deciding on the appropriate action.
- Giving the appropriate response.

Immediately you can see that you have the four skills of *listening* (a physical and communication skill), *identifying* (an evaluative skill), *deciding* (another evaluative skill), and *responding* (another physical and communication skill). What this process does not tell you is *how good* your skills were. You may listen, but not attentively enough, so you have to ask the caller to repeat the question; or you may listen but not understand what is being asked of you. Similarly with identifying and deciding, you may have misunderstood what the nature of the problem was and consequently decided on the wrong action to be taken. And finally, in your response to the caller you may not have got your message across either in the right manner or in a way that could be understood clearly.

> How well you use your skills is the key to your competence.

So how can you be objective about your level of competence, or your performance, if you prefer to think about it in this way? If you are honest with yourself you will know whether you were good or bad, but merely to say so does not prove anything, either to yourself or anyone else who might be interested – such as a future employer. If we go back to the example of our helpline contact, the proof of competence might be for example:

- 30 calls taken every hour (on average)
- 25 queries answered directly
- 5 queries referred to supervisor
- 0 repeat calls from dissatisfied customer
- 0 instances of retraining from supervisor
- 0 subsequent letters of complaint.

In other words, you were quick at understanding what the caller wanted; you made the right decisions about who should deal with the query; and where you dealt with the query yourself you provided the right information in the right way.

The ultimate proof of your competence would be if you received a bonus, promotion or additional duties and responsibilities. When you are completing Worksheet 13, you need to find some way of verifying your claims as to your level of competence. You will notice that you will need to complete a separate sheet for each duty or responsibility to give yourself sufficient room to identify *all* the skills you brought to that particular part of your job.

Worksheet 13: Occupational skills audit

Title of job:

Duty or responsibility:

The skills I used were:

What was my level of competence?

How can I prove this?

It is entirely up to you how far you want to take this process back through your employment history. But it is important to look in depth at skills you have used in all your full-time jobs, as well as any lesser jobs which you feel are personally important for one reason or another. Only by going through this process thoroughly will you begin to see if there are recurring patterns of skills being used and to what level.

Finally, when you have completed your analysis, combine all the skills you have identified from your employment history and put them in a simple list format under your PRP heading 'Occupational skills' set up as suggested on page 47.

Summary

Chapter 3 looked at the broad range of skills you might find in the workplace.

- You were encouraged to start thinking about what skills you might have from your own experience.
- You began by recording any occupational qualifications you might have.
- You made a record of your work history to include one-line statements on your duties and responsibilities for each job.
- You were introduced to workstyle categories under the broad descriptive headings of *Thinking, Organising, Administering* and *Doing*.
- The impact of computer literacy skills was touched on.
- You considered the concept of spheres of work and the skills likely to be found in them.
- You were asked to think about the type of skills you acquired from employment.
- By completing an occupational skills audit, you were able to define these skills more specifically and make judgements on your level of competence in them.

CHAPTER 4

Valuing Home-based Skills

This chapter should be compulsory reading for *everyone*: home-based skills are not just about housework and what might traditionally be regarded as 'women's work', they are about *all* the skills which are routinely carried out by men and women in and around the home. These are the third set of planks in your life raft.

There are, however, valid reasons for looking in depth at the skills traditionally associated with women. As we saw on page 16 of Chapter 1, there is a lot more to shopping than you might expect, and the skills you need to do it well are surprisingly marketable in the world of work.

The changing role of women

It is precisely because so much of what we do in and around our homes is on a daily basis that the skills we use are regarded as commonplace. As a result they tend to be undervalued – and those who use them most tend to be undervalued as well. Historically it has been women who have nurtured the hearth and home and brought up families. During the last century this role gradually changed, initially because of the demands of two world wars, and later through choice or economic necessity. In the UK, women began to leave the home to join the paid workforce in increasingly large numbers so that by the beginning of the new century they now make up around 50 per cent.

But attitudes die hard. For decades, having home-based skills was not thought of as being relevant to the workplace unless you were to be employed in domestic service or related employment, and these jobs were always in the low-status low-pay category. Women who had never worked outside the home, or who had briefly worked before bringing up a family, were unlikely to find employment in more prestigious positions.

> Our society associates status with earnings.

If you have never been employed, or only able to obtain employment in low-grade jobs with low pay and therefore low status, you are more likely to suffer from low self-esteem, a loss of self-confidence and poor levels of self-assertiveness. One of the saddest statements in recruitment interviews is the almost shame-faced apology, 'I'm only a housewife'.

For the generation of young women entering the workforce now, this is less likely to be a problem. More women are putting off having families until they have put their careers firmly in place; some are deciding against having families at all, and family structures are changing too. But for those who had their families before starting work, or took a career break and now want to return, the old problems of how home-based skills are perceived are still there.

Over the course of this chapter, we will be delving into the hidden skills we all have as we go about our daily lives, and thinking about how these can be transferred into the world of paid employment as recognised skills within the workplace. By using this approach the following truth should become clear.

> Someone who can manage and maintain a home efficiently will make a first-class employee.

And from taking this on board, it becomes possible to increase levels of confidence and the sense of self-worth.

Open a new file with the heading 'Home-based skills' and leave the page blank until you have gone through the processes needed to identify them.

The complexities of running a home

To start with we will be looking at the three areas which broadly define the types of activity associated with running a home. These are:

◆ maintaining a home
◆ managing a household
◆ caring and supporting roles.

We will then look at the skills involved in each category and show how these can relate to the world of work.

Maintaining a home

Maintaining a home to a high standard does *not* mean there isn't a speck of dust to be seen and the place has all the sterility of a show house. A house is not necessarily a home. A home is where people are comfortable and happy, but where order exists to a level where chaos is held at bay for the benefit of everyone. Housework as an end in itself can become obsessive, ritualistic and mentally suffocating, leaving no room for expansion into other activities which can bring the positive benefits of stimulation and variation to everyday life. The same can be true of the compulsive DIY fanatic, gardener or car-tinkerer.

A 'home' for the purposes of this chapter is the building itself, the contents within it, the car in the garage, and the area of land outside which belongs to the building. If you haven't got a garden or a car then you can skip over any references to them if you wish – or you can consider the implications of what is being said in case you end up with both in the future.

The areas for our skills search are therefore:

- house maintenance
- contents maintenance
- garden maintenance
- car maintenance.

You will see immediately from the above list that the topic of home maintenance is all-inclusive, even in the more traditional sense of who does what – the largely female contribution to the home contents, the female/male contribution to the building and garden, and largely male contribution to car maintenance. Today's lifestyles result in these distinctions becoming increasingly blurred with less emphasis on clear-cut divisions of labour.

> Who does what is now far more likely to be based on who is available at the time the 'what' needs doing.

House maintenance

This section looks at activities involved in keeping a house structurally sound and enhancing its appearance. Most of the skills could be described as DIY and all require the essential skills of dexterity and good hand/eye coordination. Because they are DIY, the knowledge is assumed to be basic. More sophisticated work would need the input of a professionally qualified tradesman. So if you are, or have been, employed in any of the house maintenance trades, these skills should be part of your occupational skills audit and not included for consideration here.

Where DIY is referred to here it is **not** intended to include the making of any item to your own design from scratch: this aspect is reserved for consideration in Chapter 5 when hobbies are explored in detail.

Decorating

This job comprises several sequential processes: the preparation of surfaces; the actual decorating with paint, paper, etc. and the finishing off, putting back fixtures and fittings and cleaning brushes and tools. It also demands creative skills in some cases, such as fixing patterned tiles or stencil work.

Good decorating must involve good planning and an understanding of the materials you use. Without these skills the finished effect can look shoddy, or the work has to be repeated because the sequence of stages was not thought through properly and the earlier work is damaged or spoilt. But planning is not just about getting the sequences right, it is also about adding in a realistic timescale for each sequence. You have to know all about how long different materials take to dry before you can repeat a process, or go on to the next.

Decorating also involves basic numeracy skills to work out how much paper, tiling or paint is needed to complete the job. Not paying attention to this aspect can result in having too much or too little; in wasting money or finding you can't finish the job with the materials you started with.

Repairing

Repairing is all about understanding what needs to be done to effect a repair and how to go about it using the right tools or fixatives. As with decorating, the preparation is as important as the action itself. But unlike decorating, which has a definite end point, repair work is not complete until the repair has been tested and proved to be successful. So there is the additional skill of knowing how to check accurately in the first place and then subsequently monitoring the repair to ensure it is still functioning properly.

Building

Building in this context is not meant to include large-scale projects such as extensions to the house, but rather the smaller-scale building works such as retaining walls for flower beds, paths, patios and the like.

Like decorating, building in this case includes an element of design work: the shape of the patio; the height of the wall, and the type of materials to be used. So there are not just practical basic skills in evidence but creative ones as well. And as with decorating, understanding the materials you are using and calculating the quantities needed is just as important to the success of the job.

Plumbing

Plumbing at a basic level can be tackled by most DIY fans. Changing washers, replacing ball-cocks and unblocking drains or gutters doesn't require specialist knowledge or any more specialised tools than would be found in the average home toolkit.

There is nothing creative about plumbing at this level: it is a matter of understanding how water is piped into a house, where the stop-taps are located and how to use a limited range of tools to solve problems. But it nonetheless remains a skill if you don't need to call in a specialist to solve the problem for you.

Electrical work

Electrical work in this context is limited to mending fuses and rewiring plugs.

All electrical appliances sold now come with a plug ready fitted, but there are always the occasions where flexes get rubbed and need replacing, so this skill is still useful. Similarly, modern fuse boxes have trip switches, but not every home has one, so this is another skill which still has an important role to play.

Like basic plumbing, there is nothing creative about fixing a plug, but a good deal of manual dexterity is needed, and of course, the essential understanding of how electricity works and the potentially lethal consequences of faulty connections.

Thinking Slot 9
◆ List the skills you would need to fix a shelf to a wall.

Contents maintenance

This section looks at areas of activity which involve keeping the inside of the house clean and in good order on a regular basis, as well as the maintenance and making of clothes and furnishings. Some of the activities overlap into hobbies, which we will be discussing further in the next chapter, but in this context they are activities which are carried out as part of homemaking.

Cleaning

This usually comes under the umbrella term of 'housework' and often attracts down-beat descriptive words or phrases such as 'chore' or 'daily grind'. Put simply, cleaning is the removal of dirt or dust from all the surfaces in the house, done either by wet wiping, dry wiping, sweeping or suction, and to do it correctly requires an appreciation of which method is the most appropriate for the purpose.

All cleaning requires the use of at least one piece of equipment, even if this is nothing more than a duster. In the case of wet wiping, this usually needs the addition of a cleaning agent, and it is extremely important to know how to use this correctly, particularly if you are dealing with something as dangerous as bleach. So being able to follow instructions is one of the more obvious skills involved here.

With suction cleaning, the equipment is electrical and usually has a variety of attachments for different functions dependent on the type of vacuum being used. Keeping the vacuum in good working order by frequent emptying is part of the job; so is checking that its cable and plug are in good repair.

The skills needed for cleaning are basic. The level to which we use them can be gauged by simple inspection, i.e. the lack of tide-marks in baths and cobwebs on the ceiling – or perhaps the existence of them. Like decorating, to be effective cleaning has to be done methodically and in an order which will not involve spoiling any of the areas already cleaned.

Thinking Slot 10

◆ Describe the different stages of your cleaning programme and consider what this tells you about the way you approach basic but essential tasks.

Laundering and ironing

Not many of us have to wash our clothes in the kitchen sink anymore: an exhausting, usually very sweaty business which could take a full day to complete. Now it has become more of a trial of strength with a machine and an array of options, few of which seem to tie in precisely with the helpful labels on our clothes. There is the 'red sock' syndrome to be avoided with the need for careful sorting and dividing of different fabrics into different washing cycles; the selection of the appropriate program; the right amount of washing powder and softener to put into the right compartment; and crucially,   the knowledge of how to start the machine, how to manually intervene where necessary, and ultimately, how to open it.

What was a very basic activity in the past involving mainly physical stamina has now become a complex series of processes requiring an ability to understand and translate (often literally) the manufacturer's instructions and put them into practice. It is no different from machine minding in a factory.

Ironing, when a fabric demands it, remains a skill which requires a methodical approach and manual dexterity. The iron itself may have become more sophisticated (with its choice of temperatures and on/off steam button), so that it is important to understand what combination to choose for different fabrics – but it is still an iron and, like any tool, the quality of the result will depend on how skilful its operator is in using it, and on good hand/eye coordination.

Sewing and mending

We are looking at sewing in the creative sense in this section, not as a hobby but as a homemaking activity, possibly where it is important to save both time and money. There are two types of sewing to consider:

◆ by hand; and
◆ by machine,

and they are two very different skills. The first requires a basic knowledge of the variety of stitches available; which are the most appropriate for the job expected of them; good hand/eye coordination; an ability to produce standard stitch lengths, and dexterity. The second introduces all the skills necessary for operating a machine: understanding how it works, setting it up, and basic maintenance. Added to these are then the additional skills of foot or knee control to operate the machine, dexterity, and good hand/eye coordination.

There are also the skills associated with what is being sewed. Making clothes from patterns, like putting together a flat-pack wardrobe, demands that you follow the instructions precisely. But unlike putting together the wardrobe where all the pieces are pre-made, there are additional skills such as measuring; choosing the right material; understanding how patterns have to be laid out on the cloth; how the cloth has to be cut and marked correctly; how button holes have to be made; how zips are fitted; how adjustments are made to the basic pattern etc. These skills are all about craftsmanship.

Making curtains or other furnishings needs similar skills and attention to detail, such as lining up patterns to match.

Mending is perhaps a skill less in evidence than it used to be. We tend to throw out socks with holes in or trousers torn at the knee, and buy new ones. But simple sewing repairs to hems or seams still have their place.

Garden maintenance

This section considers the various activities which occupy us outside the house. The 'garden' for our purposes can be anything from a window box in a small yard area to the more spacious variety usually associated with TV gardening programmes. All the skills are manual, with additional skills tagged on to them.

Propagating, planting and tending

Propagating skills apply whether you pop your seeds into potting compost in a margerine tub, cover it with cling film and leave it on a window sill, or have the luxury of proper seed trays and a greenhouse. Knowing the right conditions and the right location for planting different plant species, and being able to do all the right things at the right times so that they thrive and bear fruit, or flowers, or just stay healthy, are skills the professional gardener picks up, either through practice or study, or both.

Maintaining healthy plants also involves combatting insects and disease and being able to handle the substances (chemical or biological) which are used for the purpose. This includes following instructions on their use, measuring quantities correctly and storing them properly.

Designing

Designing a garden is a creative skill. You can design it on paper, drawing it out to scale if this is important, or you can plunge straight into the job and mark everything out by the peg-and-string method. But regardless of which way you complete your design, you are creating something and using all the skills found in *any* creative task: visualising what the outcome will be; planning where specific details will be placed; putting your ideas into practice, with any necessary second thoughts where appropriate, and seeing the design through to completion. And because you are designing a garden and not a house, you are also bringing to your design work the skills needed to make plants thrive in the positions you have allocated for them.

Don't forget, landscape gardening and garden design are skills which lead to both employment and self-employment.

Maintaining garden structures

Garden structures, like houses, do not look after themselves: greenhouses have to be cleaned and fumigated; sheds, summerhouses and wooden fences need treating with preservatives on a regular basis; seats need varnish or paint, and the sundial and terrace need a good scrub to get rid of moss and algae. In other words, this type of maintenance requires the skills needed when you decorate, clean or repair the house.

Looking after livestock

Livestock in this context can be the wild birds on the bird feeder outside your window, the goldfish in the pond by the terrace, or the birds in your aviary/pigeon loft/hen coop at the bottom of the garden.

Many of the skills needed to be successful are the same as those you would apply to looking after the domestic animals in your home, or even those of parenting. They are caring skills overlaid with the additional skills of knowing how to feed animals correctly, and in cases where they are not wild, how to handle them and tend to their needs. There are obvious connections between these skills and those required in jobs associated with animal husbandry.

Maintaining tools and machinery

If you have an area outside the house to look after, you need tools and equipment for the job: spades, forks, trowels, lawnmowers, shears, pruners, chainsaws, rotavators etc. The tools require little maintenance apart from being kept clean and, in the case of any moving parts, regular oiling. Machines on the other hand need to be maintained, both on the occasions when they are used and, like cars, when they need a more thorough overhaul.

As with earlier sections on the topic of maintenance, we are only looking at basic maintenance here; not stripping down a machine to its component parts and reassembling. If you can do this type of maintenance confidently and efficiently and are self-taught as well, then highlight this facet of your ability: being able to teach yourself skills is a valuable skill in itself. However, if you can carry out maintenance as a result of existing or previous employment as a mechanic, then don't record your skills here but in your occupational skills audit.

Basic maintenance is about understanding the needs of your machine while you are using it: how much petrol or oil it takes, and what type; how long the battery takes to recharge; which parts need regular oiling; what parts need cleaning after use and how this is done.

Using some machines, like chainsaws for example, may require special equipment or clothing, and even personal instruction on how to use them safely. Even if your advice session is quite brief, if you are then able to use the machinery correctly and safely, you have just acquired a new skill.

Car maintenance

There are two levels of car maintenance:
- basic checks (oil, tyres and lights);
- servicing (wheel changes, bodywork repairs, oil changes, etc.).

As responsible car owners we should all carry out the basic checks as a matter of course. It is easy to scoff at how simple these actions are, but they still require knowledge and skill to complete them successfully: reading the manual; knowing where the dip stick is and where the oil level should be; being able to take a tyre pressure reading and pump up a tyre to the required pressure; and checking that all the lights work correctly. And just like the skills of cleaning in the house, cleaning and washing the car demand the same methodical approach, use of equipment and cleaners.

Servicing is a more sophisticated level of maintenance and not one regularly undertaken by most people. If you are able to carry out this type of maintenance successfully, then you obviously have a far greater range of skills – ones which can be easily transferred into employment. The comments made earlier on machine maintenance skills apply equally in this case.

Thinking Slot 11
- Make a list of jobs which include skills used in basic home maintenance.

Managing a household

> Skills required to manage a home are indisputably, as the term suggests, managerial.

This is what makes them so important and potentially useful as employment skills.

Managing a household successfully combines the complexities of:

- leadership
- time management
- forward planning
- financial control
- organisational and administrative skills

and most important of all:

- a wide range of communication skills, i.e.
  - listening carefully

   – speaking effectively face-to-face and over the phone
   – negotiating and diplomacy
   – persuading and commanding
   – the ability to formulate and write official letters.

In Chapter 1 when 'shopping' was considered in some detail, we saw how completing this apparently mundane task successfully involved a broad range of embryonic management skills. In the remainder of this section, we will see how the lists of skills set out above are mirrored in miniature in many of our routine activities in the home.

Leading others

We looked at some of the leadership skills of 'advising', 'persuading' and 'instructing' under the heading 'Dealing with people or animals' in Chapter 3 pages 52–53.

In a household which comprises more than one person, someone will always surface who takes charge of a situation. It may be the same person in every situation, or there may be a fluid arrangement whereby different people take the lead to match the occasion, but there is usually one person more capable of dealing with a particular set of circumstances than anyone else, i.e. possessing the qualities of a 'leader'.

Your leadership style can be both active and passive: you can tell everyone what to do and when to do it, even in the nicest possible way; or you can be approached by others who ask you for your help or guidance. If the outcome of your actions is that others do what you have told them to do or suggested they do, you are a leader and others are prepared to defer to, or be guided by, your authority.

Managing time and planning ahead

> If you manage your time well, things you plan to do get done.

In the context of the home, time management goes on without benefit of such a sophisticated label. You either plan, or know you have to do, a list of things within a timescale. After dropping the children off at school, you will have just enough time to buy in the groceries, collect the vacuum from the repair shop and be back home for the expected phone call. And so it goes on, day in and day out, the interweaving of a whole range of different activities within a more rigid framework of external time limitations, whether these are imposed by school hours or work hours.

Forward planning can be part of this structure, arranging for particular events to take place at suitable times within your day. It usually involves keeping a diary of some sort to keep track of what is happening. And the diary may not just involve your own activities, but those of other members of the household as well: parent-teacher meetings, ballet classes, football matches, arrangements to eat out with friends – they are all relevant. Planning and preparing meals (including shopping) should also be included in the forward planning category, as well as all the complex preparations needed for a family holiday – the ultimate logistical nightmare.

If you put these skills into an employment context you can see quite easily how important they are to the smooth running of any business.

Controlling finance

Financial control can include budgeting, keeping an eye on the cash flow, paying bills – whether these are one-offs or regular payments such as the mortgage, rent, insurance premiums, council tax, fuel or phone bills, credit card accounts and savings plans. To be successful the system has to include accurate record keeping of income and expenditure. It also needs built-in safeguards to allow sufficient funds to be kept in reserve for the unexpected as well as the planned-for costs such as having to buy a new washing machine or Christmas and birthday presents. A monitoring process also has to be in place to make sure the system works and the household does not overspend.

It is worth remembering that just like the home, no business can succeed without the skills of good financial management.

Organising and administering

Organisational skills in the home are likely to be the active, participative type of skills where you make sure that what has to be done is done, or has been done. In other words, it is forward planning put into action.

Cooking is a skill which can fall into this category, although there is a large slice of time management involved as well, since meals usually have to be ready by a certain time to fit into the household's schedule. There are also creative skills involved. Cooking is all about organising a vast array of different ingredients in different ways to produce different meals. It involves understanding the nutritional value of foods; how ingredients can be combined; the various methods of cooking; using the right utensils and equipment; maintaining equipment; following recipes and creating your own.

A more obvious example of pure organising skill is the family holiday. It is usually done over a period of several weeks involving a series of preparations. There are lists to be drawn up of what has to be taken; new clothes to be bought; existing ones to be laundered; toiletries to be selected; equipment to be checked (cameras, car rack, skis, radios etc.); documentation to be obtained and put in a safe place (passports, tickets, medical insurance and so on); the dog to be booked into kennels; the fridge to be emptied gradually; the neighbourhood watch coordinator to be notified nearer the time; milk and papers to be cancelled; travel arrangements checked, and at some point, everyone else to be organised too.

If you get it all right, you would have no problems in any job requiring good organisatonal skills.

Administration is a more passive skill – the combination of a little financial control, organisational input and the art of paper-pushing to good effect. It can involve the maintenance of household records from bank statements to school reports; the running of systems to ensure regular checks take place, whether these are medical or dental appointments, or servicing contract renewals; the ordering or reordering of household requirements such as heating oil or coal, or anything which involves filling out a form, whether this is an income tax return or the register of electors.

Like organisational skills, good administrative skills are needed for any successful business or organisation.

Communicating with everyone

If ever there was a pivotal management skill, it has got to be good communicating abilities: without these it is impossible to manage anyone. And if there is one area where it is possible to really hone up on your communication skills it is in managing a household, because here there are so many points of contact with other people. Besides all the individuals who make up your household and extended family, there are a huge number of outsiders who will touch your life at some time or another: officials of every description, the medical and teaching professionals, tradespeople, sales people, neighbours, friends, acquaintances and complete strangers.

We have already considered some of these skills in Chapter 3 when we were looking at employment skills under the headings 'Serving', 'Communicating', 'Persuading', 'Advising' and 'Instructing'. Getting along with people regardless of their opinions or what status they hold is another communication skill – diplomacy. Getting them to accept your argument and take on board your point of view, or you theirs is yet another – the ability to negotiate successfully.

> Good verbal communication skills depend on having finely tuned mental antennae.

This means how quickly you can pick up the clues by reading body language, tone of voice, and the type of vocabulary used, and then how quickly you can adapt your own reactions to achieve the appropriate response for the occasion. To some extent this demands some role-play as well, since in order to achieve your desired outcome you may find it necessary to mask your real reaction with another. We all do it, sometimes automatically. We adopt authority roles with children, but often find ourselves playing more subservient roles with our parents. With our peer group, with people we don't know, with professionals in positions of authority, we often adopt completely different personae to match the circumstances we are in at the time.

Managing a household also requires good writing skills. Closely linked to administrative skills, the ability to write well-structured formal letters is needed when dealing with official bodies or institutions. Letters involve not only the basic literacy skill of writing itself and the conventions of layout and style, but also the additional skills of typewriting or word processing. These additional skills are immediately identifiable as abilities capable of being transferred into the workplace.

Thinking Slot 12
◆ List the basic management skills have you used today in your home.

Caring and supporting roles

Caring and supporting in the home can involve looking after children, adults or both. Households are not static entities: they grow, age and ultimately break up, either because of death or separation. Learning to cope with the different stages of a household's development often demands high levels of input and patience, understanding, and the willingness to devote time and effort. These are caring skills.

Parenting

The most obvious caring and supporting role in the home environment is that of parenting. Parenting skills vary with the age of the child. During early childhood the skills are in response to basic human needs, such as:

◆ feeding
◆ clothing and
◆ bathing

and we can handle these because we already have the skills to understand the need for food, warmth and hygiene in our own lives.

Additional skills are those of:

◆ protecting and
◆ nursing

which are the nurturing skills associated with giving the child a safe environment in which to thrive by guarding against potential safety hazards in and around the home, and those of recognising the signs of illness, which can either be treated by yourself or need the input of professional help. Nursing a child often involves understanding how to administer medication safely. Some parents acquire a higher level of nursing skills with children who suffer from ailments which demand regular attention, such as diabetes where an ability to administer insulin by injection is needed.

As children grow up however, a different type of skill has to be introduced, becoming more sophisticated and refined as the child becomes an adolescent and then a young adult. These skills include:

- advising
- guiding
- supporting
- encouraging
- teaching.

These are clearly recognisable as abilities which demand a high level of communication skills and interpersonal skills, i.e. those skills which help individuals in society interrelate with others.

What is probably overlooked in the gradual process of parenting over the space of eighteen years or so is the simple fact that, by successfully bringing up a child, you have probably developed a whole portfolio of skills you never realised you had in the first place. In the world of work this process is often given the grandiose title 'Continuing Professional (or Personal) Development'.

Childcare is set to become one of the fastest growing employment sectors with the increase in the number of mothers returning to the workplace who need childcare facilities for young children. People providing childcare facilities are being encouraged to undertake training to raise standards in this sector. Training providers have developed programmes leading to National Vocational Qualifications (NVQs) in Early Years' Care and Education. These training programmes are aimed at people caring for children not only in playgroups, nurseries, crèches and after-school clubs, but also childminding in their own home, and can apply to both paid and unpaid work situations.

One such training provider is the Centre for Continuing Education, Training and Development (CETAD), based at Lancaster University. CETAD received recognition as an Investor in People (IIP) in 1994 and again in 1998. Around a thousand people every year take CETAD training courses in a range of vocational subjects and 80 per cent find paid employment at the end of their programmes.

In conjunction with Training and Enterprise Councils (TECs), and Local Enterprise Companies (LECs) in Scotland, CETAD provides individually tailored programmes where they are needed. CETAD is prepared to put together training programmes in any centre of population where ten or more people are interested in obtaining recognised training and can often help in accessing funding where this is needed. Full details of how to contact CETAD appear in the Useful Addresses section on page 187.

Being a carer

Caring and supporting in the home is not of course restricted to parenting. There are around 600,000 people in the UK who spend their lives looking after relatives of all ages who are either permanently ill or impaired by physical or mental incapacities.

There is such a huge range of problems being coped with by carers that it is impossible here to identify all the skills needed. If you are a carer yourself, however, simply listing all the things you do using -*ing* words will give you some idea of the extent of your talents. Your experience would undoubtedly be transferable into circumstances where others could benefit from your knowledge and expertise.

Caring for the elderly

As a society we are seeing an increasing number of people living well into their eighties and nineties. Our expectations of three-score-years-and-ten are now regularly surpassed. The effects of our living longer, combined with a greater emphasis on keeping the very elderly out of old-style institutions, means that there is an increasing number of people who are not only looking after their children, but their parents as well.

Some of the skills used for parenting are those needed for looking after elderly relatives as well, for instance:

- nursing
- tending to personal needs
- administering first aid and medication.

Skills in looking after the elderly can provide the basis for paid employment in the same way as childcare skills. Training providers, such as CETAD mentioned earlier in this chapter, run programmes for people wanting to improve their skills or have them formally recognised through certification or NVQs. Not everyone goes 'dotty' in their old age or slips into 'second childhood'. Today, many elderly people are more mentally and physically agile than was the case when their own parents were their age, so 'caring' can have a wide range of meanings. On the one hand you may well be looking after someone in your own home who needs 24-hour care; on the other, however, your parents may not be living with you, but you may be needed occasionally to help out with the decorating, heavy shopping or to sort out a tax return. So caring skills when dealing with the elderly are not as neatly packaged as you might expect and can overlap other home-based skills such as house maintenance and financial control.

To many elderly people, an often overlooked skill is that of allowing them their independence of thought and action to do what they can within their capabilities. In other words, respecting them as individuals.

Thinking Slot 13
- Make a list of your caring skills.

Drawing up your home-based skills audit

At this stage, you should be feeling more confident about how to identify your skills, and will no longer need such detailed help in recording them, or in recognising ways of proving your competence. However, you have probably found that you have so many skills to think about you may easily overlook some of them. It may be helpful therefore to complete a weekly logsheet of activities over a four-week period, or longer if you think this is more appropriate.

The suggested layout in Worksheet 14 divides the day into three-hour periods in which you can record your activities. This not only provides a useful way of preventing you accidentally overlooking something important, but also gives you an immediate overview of which activities are the predominant ones. The skills involved in these are therefore likely to be more advanced either through regular usage or because you have become more adept at using them.

Worksheet 14: Home-based activities: Weekly logsheet

	Sun	Mon	Tues	Wed	Thur	Fri	Sat
6–9 a.m.							
9–12 noon							
12–3 p.m.							
3–6 p.m.							
6–9 p.m.							
9–12 mid.							
12–6 a.m.							

To pick up the non-weekly activities in your home life, check through your diary and extract details of anything you believe reflects some aspect of home-based skills. Note these down as a separate list on Worksheet 15.

Worksheet 15 : Home-based activities: Non-weekly

Occasional:

Monthly:

Quarterly:

Six-monthly:

All your home-based activities can now be transferred to separate audit worksheets as single entities, and the list of skills you need to complete them noted underneath, in the same way as discussed under 'Tackling your occupational skills audit' in Chapter 3 (page 61). A suggested layout is given in Worksheet 16.

Worksheet 16 : Home-based skills audit

Activity:

The skills I used were:

My level of competence was:

How can I prove this?

Finally, condense your skills into a simple category list and enter this under your 'Home-based skills' heading on the page you set up at the start of this section.

Summary

Chapter 4 considered the many different skills which you acquire and use on a regular basis in and around the home, but which you may not have recognised earlier as having much significance.

- You were introduced to the three main areas of *Maintaining a home, Managing a household* and *Caring and supporting roles* and the skills likely to be found in each of these categories.
- Through the use of Thinking Slots you were encouraged to think about your home-based skills in a different light.
- By completing Worksheets you were able to identify the activities you are involved in.
- As part of the skills audit, you identified the skills you used in these activities.
- You were also asked to find ways of proving your level of competence in these skills.

CHAPTER 5

Exploring Pastime Skills

I n this last of the chapters looking into the different areas of your life and the skills to be found there, we will be investigating the life skills you use in your pastimes. These are the last set of planks you need for constructing your life raft.

Chapter 1 introduced the idea of thinking about your pastime skills in a new way: as signposts pointing to the right sort of job for you. They are good signposts as you do what you do in your spare time because you *want* to do it, not because you *have* to. The motivation comes from within yourself.

You were also shown the value of dividing your spare-time activities into the three categories:

- ◆ hobbies
- ◆ leisure pursuits
- ◆ voluntary work.

Considering spare-time activities

The reason for breaking down your activities into these separate groupings is to provide a basis for recognising the different motivational drives behind what you do: it provides you with the opportunity to realise you have certain preferences when you make decisions about how you want to spend your spare time. This approach will be important to you if you are starting to think about taking a career break on a temporary basis or leaving the workforce completely.

The most common reason for taking a career break is to start a family. If you don't intend to return to work straightaway, the break in work patterns provides you with the chance to review your future, and the breathing space to make new plans. Looking at your previous spare-time activities can often provide you with some answers.

If your career break is likely to be permanent, either because of health problems or retirement, how you spend your newly acquired spare time can make all the difference between an interesting and stimulating period of your life, and becoming a couch potato. With the possibility of up to 40 or 50 years still ahead of you, these years should be ones which offer the freedom to be yourself, to enjoy new experiences, or perhaps to resurrect old interests.

So whether you are wondering if you are in the right job, taking a career break or thinking about what you can do once you are no longer working, your starting point is here.

We begin with the now familiar method of recording facts as base reference points from which to work. We will then think about what skills can be identified from the different types of pastimes before going on to complete a skills audit.

Remember as you progress, *do include* all the pastimes you have followed over the years. Part of the process of investigating your various skills is to identify any you may have had in the past which you have allowed to slip into disuse, as well as those you have carried on using over the passage of time.

Begin as you have done with earlier audits by opening a new file with a blank page, this time with the heading 'Pastime skills'.

Spotting skills in hobbies

> Hobbies are the pastimes where you are motivated to *do* something.

With a hobby you are actively involved in a way which gives you a sense of personal satisfaction and achievement. We will look at three different categories of hobbies:

- membership of formal groups, e.g. clubs, societies, etc.,
- membership of informal groups, and
- solitary hobbies,

and these will each be divided into active hobbies and sedentary hobbies.

When you come to complete your record of hobbies (particularly under the heading 'Formal groups') don't include any active membership of charities or other organisations dedicated to providing services to adults, children or animals –

Red Cross, Mencap, RSPCA, Lepra, or the Scouts for instance. For the purposes of this exercise, these groups should appear under the heading 'Voluntary work', *not* 'Hobbies.

Membership of formal groups

Formal groups in this context mean that the organisation you belong to has either a formal constitution, or a group of people who act as officers, such as secretary and treasurer. These organisations can include sports clubs, operatic, music and dramatic societies, political parties, religious groups (devoted to religious study rather than providing some form of help to the community), and so on.

From the list of possible organisations under this heading, there are those which could be described as involving robust physical activities as an integral part of their function (sports clubs are the most obvious). Others, such as political parties or music societies, are in essence groups where the activities are much more likely to be based on meetings, lectures, concerts etc.

Worksheet 17 is suggested for you to complete to record your membership of both types of formal group. If you have a mix of physical and non-physical activities, record the physical activities on a separate worksheet and head this up as Worksheet 17(A). If you hold, or held, one of the official positions in any organisation, including being a member of the committee, record this in the final column. Noting any positions held in an organisation is important because this demonstrates that you have specific skills associated with the position itself. As you can probably see immediately, these are types of organisational skills which can be transferred into other situations, and would have particular interest to potential future employers, or other organisations looking for expertise.

Worksheet 17: Membership of formal groups: Non-physical activities
(***Note***: Use this format if needed for Worksheet 17(A): Membership of formal groups: Physical activities)

Name of club	From	To	Type of activity and any positions held

Formal group skills

Formal groups tend to operate within a recognisable hierarchy with the committee and officers at the top of the tree. Being an ordinary member would not involve you in the running of the organisation as much as taking part in its activities.

The obvious skills you might expect to have as an ordinary member would be directly related to the activity of the group. These are most likely to be physical skills overlaid with additional attributes. As a member of an operatic society, for instance, your first skill is likely to be the ability to sing in tune. But you may also be able to play an instrument and you would almost certainly be expected to be at least reasonably competent at acting. Ancillary skills could also include creative skills such as costume design, set making, lighting design (not forgetting the all-important skill of directing), and the technical skills necessary for stage management or operating a computerised lighting board.

As well as these individual skills, you are also likely to need the interpersonal skills associated with any group activity:

◆   the ability to work with others;
◆   communication skills;
◆   leadership skills (as a team captain or choral leader for instance);

and if you are part of the group's organisational structure as well, you could also have:

◆   organisational and administrative skills;
◆   leadership skills (in your capacity as an official);
◆   management skills.

From earlier exercises, you will also know that you can break down these very broad skills categories into their component skills.

Thinking Slot 14

◆   From your list of formal group activities, are your skills mainly physical/technical/creative/organisational/managerial?

Membership of informal groups

Informal groups for the purpose of this exercise are groups which comprise like-minded individuals, who meet to pursue a particular activity on a regular basis. The group should be fluid, with no visible hierarchy, and membership consists of friends and acquaintances. You belong to this category if for instance you are part of a rock or jazz band, a choral group, a cycling or riding or walking group, or dance club. The criteria would also include a group of friends who meet regularly to surf the Net at a cybercafé, give readings of their written work, or engage in political or philosophical argument.

To be meaningful for the purposes of a skills audit, your membership of a group of this nature should have lasted for at least a year. You can make an exception for yourself if you were unable to continue due to unforeseen circumstances and feel that your membership played an important part in your life.

From the examples listed, you can see that informal groups can also be divided into the more or less physical in content, but they still retain the vital ingredient of *doing something.*

As you did with the formal group, repeat the process for your informal group membership, completing separate worksheets for the different types of group – physical and non-physical – remembering to include past and present membership so that you have a complete picture.

Worksheet 18: Membership of informal groups: Non-physical activities
(Note: Use this format if needed for Worksheet 18(A): Membership of informal groups: Physical activities)

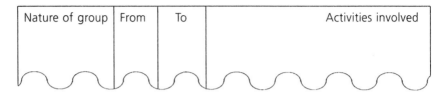

Nature of group	From	To	Activities involved

Informal group skills

The personal skills you bring to an informal group will depend entirely on the activity the group enjoys. They can be the physical skills of cycling, dancing or walking, or the more sophisticated skills of being able to play a musical instrument, or engage in philosophical debate. The range of possibilities is enormous.

Because there is no rigid hierarchy in an informal group, the skills associated with an organisational type of structure are not relevant. But you are very much part of a team, however loosely that terminology can be applied. Under these circumstances you would expect to find interpersonal skills as the most important feature, acting as the glue to keep the group together. These interpersonal skills are the same as those for formal groupings:

+ an ability to work with others;
+ good communication skills.

Unlike formal groups, however, where a leader is selected (e.g. a team captain) and the rest of the team remain subordinate, in informal groups there is the possibility of some leadership skills being called for on occasions, usually when the rest recognise that someone within the group can supply the necessary expertise to meet a particular situation. Once the situation is resolved, the leadership role ceases.

Thinking Slot 15
+ From your list of informal group activities, are your skills mainly physical/technical/creative/organisational/managerial?

Solitary hobbies

Not everyone is a team person. Many hobbies exist which are enjoyed by the individual alone and, like the previous two categories, they can be divided into the more physically demanding and the sedentary.

The range of solitary hobbies is huge. Take, for example, the solo rock climber or wind surfer at one extreme, through the jogger or recreational swimmer, the rabbit breeder or canary fancier, the DIY fanatic or gardener, the knitter or sewer, the artist or pianist, the novelist or poet, to the coin or stamp collector at the other.

In this vast sea of activity lies a wealth of talent, all of it potentially useful as a means into employment or as a source of inspiration to others.

As with the previous sections, there is a suggested worksheet for you to use when you record your solitary hobbies. Once again, complete separate sheets for your physical/non-physical categories and include all the hobbies you have ever had which lasted for at least a year or so. Any period less than this and the skills you had or developed are likely to be too transient to be useful. However, if there were circumstances which prevented you from continuing with a hobby you would definitely want to resurrect if you had more time, or money, or whatever, then make the exception and include this in your list as well.

Worksheet 19: Solitary hobbies: Non-physical activities

(Note: Use this format if needed for Worksheet 19(A): Solitary hobbies: Physical activities)

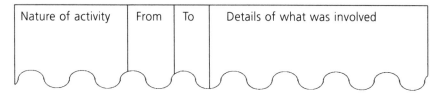

Nature of activity	From	To	Details of what was involved

Solitary hobby skills

Besides the physical skills which are part of the sports-orientated hobby, there are the creative skills of the designers; the ability to be methodical and organised if you are a collector; the technical skills of the mechanical, and the nurturing skills needed in horticulture and animal husbandry, as just some of the possibilities.

Common to all, however, is the the very strong element of self-motivation, combined with a personal level of ability which, while quite modest in some cases, can reach the dizzy heights of the expert in others. There is also the ability to learn through practice or study, so that even someone who does not have any paper qualifications may have good practical skills built up over a period of time. The ability to work on your own, to set your own standards and meet them are additional skills. These too are talents which can be used to good effect in the workplace.

The types of skills you are *unlikely* to see are the interpersonal skills of working with others, leadership or communication skills. You may in fact be quite a reserved or introspective person. This is no criticism: it's just the way you are.

Thinking Slot 16

♦ From your list of solitary hobbies, are your skills mainly physical/technical/creative/organisational?

Spotting skills in leisure pursuits

For the purposes of your skills search, your leisure pursuits, as discussed in Chapter 1 (page 17), were defined as the pursuit of leisure, and a clear distinction was made between these and active hobbies.

> In leisure pursuits your involvement is largely passive and the stimulus comes from an external input.

In other words, with the exception of a social event, such as a trip down to the local pub or a meal at a restaurant with friends, you do not take part in the action itself.

The skills associated with these pastimes are by and large at a fairly basic level, starting with the foundation skills of being able to see, hear, speak, etc. You may well have the physical, technical or creative skills which would be needed if you were taking part in the action, but because you are not these skills are not being used, so you can't say you are using them in this context: they have been relegated to the 'background knowledge' category.

To enjoy leisure pursuits, you do not require any specialist background knowledge at all. For instance, it is not essential to be knowledgeable to enjoy watching a sports match: you can enjoy it simply as an experience, from the pleasure or excitement you find in being a spectator and being entertained. Similarly, you do not need to be an artist or musician to enjoy a visit to an art exhibition or concert.

The skills you are more likely to use depend on *how* you enjoy your leisure pursuits. This distinction is important. Is the pastime spent:

1   with other people?
2   on your own?

We will look at each of these facets in turn.

Leisure time with other people

As soon as you take part in any activity where other people are involved, you need some level of interpersonal skills, i.e. your ability to get on with other people. This applies to any social grouping, formal, informal or casual.

In the context of leisure pursuits, how the casual group functions depends on the reason for the group getting together in the first place. For example, if the group is made up entirely of football supporters watching their team on TV, the sense of social cohesion will be very strong in those circumstances and there is unlikely to be any friction between members of the group. The demands on your interpersonal skills in this type of situation therefore are not very large.

At this point it is worth mentioning that if the group met on a *regular* weekly basis to *attend* the football match, rather than watch it on TV, there is an element of activity and because of this the group should be categorised as being 'informal' rather than 'casual', and should be listed under hobbies. This is because there is the likelihood that such a group would have some organisational input in order to get to the venue, and possibly some element of informal leadership over peripheral activities by the group before, during and after the match.

Not all casual groups are so cohesive however. For example, if the group meets at the local pub because they all like the ale which is served there, the attraction is the ale and not necessarily the opinions or attitudes of those who drink it. In these circumstances, the group can have a much more diverse mix and conversation and the exchange of ideas may need to be more carefully managed. This type of social setting requires a higher level of interpersonal skills, including diplomacy and negotiation.

As with the example of the football supporters, there is a point at which if the social meeting has an element of a regular activity, e.g. a game of darts or dominoes in the pub, this should be entered in your 'hobbies' section under 'Membership of informal groups'.

Having given some thought as to the right category to choose, note those pastimes you know to be leisure pursuits on suggested Worksheet 20 (page 96). You need to say how frequently you spend time 'at your leisure'. This is so that you can give recognition to the amount of time you set aside for this activity and give some quantitative value to it. You may want to record this time in hours per day, per week or per month. This is literally your 'free time', and if at some stage you have to make space in your life for other activities, this is the area you may have to plunder first to provide you with the time you need.

Worksheet 20: Leisure pursuits with other people

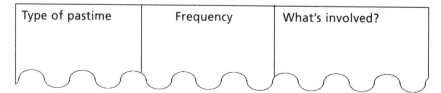

Type of pastime	Frequency	What's involved?

Leisure time on your own

In this category, there will be no interpersonal skills simply because there is no one else with you, but you are using skills nonetheless. If you watch TV, listen to the radio or hi-fi, you need at least the foundation skills which use your senses. If you read the paper or a book, then you have your reading skills to add in. (As soon as you start filling in the crossword, however, you are taking part in an activity, so this has to belong to the 'Solitary hobbies' section.)

Your ability to cope with solitude is important. For someone who cannot bear to be without people around them, this is a skill they do not have. It's interesting to note that although many job advertisements press home the need to be able to work as part of a team, there are also those which stress the ability to work on your own. If you have opted to spend your leisure time on your own it is because you enjoy, or even prefer, your own company, and this highlights a facet of your personality which could point to a preference for an individual style of working. Look back at the list you compiled under your 'Solitary hobbies' and see if there is a similar motivation here too.

It is also worth considering whether you choose to relax on your own because *you* want to choose what stimulus you pick for your entertainment, rather than have someone else impose a choice on you. This is a clear statement of being independently minded – of knowing what you want.

With these thoughts in mind, complete your list of those leisure pursuits you enjoy on your own on Worksheet 21.

Worksheet 21 : Leisure pursuits on your own

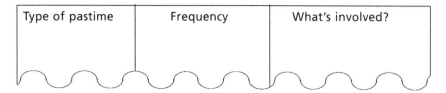

Type of pastime	Frequency	What's involved?

Spotting skills in voluntary work

The distinctions was made in Chapter 1 (pages 17–18) between hobbies and voluntary work: with the former it is you who receives the direct benefit; with the latter, it is someone else.

> Voluntary work should include your commitment to others.

For the purposes of your pastime audit, voluntary work should include any membership of, or activity in, a charity or other organisation dedicated to providing services to adults, children or animals. But in this case it should also include a separate category – your own commitment to others which does not fall within the hierarchy of a structured organisation.

Structured voluntary organisations

These organisations can range from the monolithic international charities such as Oxfam to the local cats' protection league. Like all organisations they have a recognised hierarchy of officials and committees and, depending on their size, they may even have a group of paid workers who direct and organise the thrust of the charity and manage its funds. Working for a charity in a paid capacity is employment and *not* voluntary work. Voluntary work is where you give your time and energy without payment in order to further the aims of the charity or organisation.

Your involvement can be limited to having a collecting box in your home or local shop for which you are responsible, or expanded to more demanding roles, such as helping to run a charity shop; organising an appeal mailshot; running or taking part in a fund-raising event; sitting on a committee; or being an official of the committee, i.e. chairman, secretary or treasurer.

List your involvement with the structured voluntary organisations in Worksheet 22. If you hold, or have held any official position with the organisation, this should be recorded in the final column.

Worksheet 22: Activities with voluntary organisations

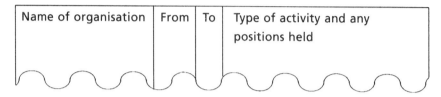

Name of organisation	From	To	Type of activity and any positions held

Skills from voluntary work with organisations

There are so many skills in this area that it is impossible to cover them all adequately. To give at least a flavour of the range of activities likely to be involved and their associated skills, let's look at what might be required to run a club. This could be a youth club, luncheon club for the elderly, drop-in centre or play group for handicapped children.

At the top of the organisation there will be an executive committee with its Chairman, Secretary and Treasurer. This group will be responsible for running the club. The Chairman will need to possess interpersonal skills, leadership qualities and to be capable of running meetings effectively. The Secretary will be responsible for official correspondence, taking, producing and distributing minutes of the meetings and providing guidance on constitutional matters and other administrative or legal requirements covering the organisation's activities. The Treasurer will need financial management skills, accounting and book-keeping skills. Committee members will be expected to have interpersonal skills associated with team working. Everyone will need good communication skills.

Some of the committee members may have individual responsibilities. Someone may take on the role of coordinator for fund-raising events. This person will need to be methodical in their approach to ensure volunteers know what they are doing, when and where, and who to report to. Good organisational abilities and communication skills are essential.

Another member may be responsible for the building the club occupies. This will call for someone capable of organising maintenance work; making sure the building is properly insured; checking that safety standards are met and fire-fighting installations are inspected; and ensuring fire drills are carried out as required.

If the club caters for people who need transport to and from the club's premises, there may be need for a transport coordinator. This person may need to negotiate with local taxi firms or coach hire companies and ensure that they are kept informed of any changes in the routes or the names of people who are to be collected. It may also be necessary to coordinate other volunteers on a rota basis to act as escorts, or even to take part in the transport arrangements as a driver.

There may also be a coordinator in overall charge of any activities when the club is open. This would need someone capable of planning a schedule of activities for club members; organising any additional help that might be required; hiring entertainers or caterers; sitting in with the executive committee at recruitment interviews for any paid staff, such as cleaners or caretakers; and, depending on the type of club, having extra communication skills necessary for a good understanding of people with hearing difficulties, those with impaired sight, young children, the elderly or handicapped. They may also need to have qualifications in first aid and be able to cope with additional difficulties arising from club members' personal hygiene requirements.

From this brief overview of our imaginary club we can see every skill needed to run a business or any other organisation: managerial, administrative, financial, organisational, supervisory, teamworking and team building, interpersonal etc.

It is possible to gain both recognition and qualifications for unpaid work in the voluntary sector, particularly where this involves giving advice and guidance. There are over two million people in this sector and training programmes are available for volunteers who want to work towards a recognised qualification – the NVQ in Advice and Guidance. The Centre for Continuing Education, Training and Development (CETAD), mentioned in Chapter 4 (page 82), provides training for volunteers working with a wide variety of voluntary organisations such as the Citizens' Advice Bureau, Samaritans, NACRO, Alzheimer's Society, MIND and Women's Aid, as part of its wider programme of developing advice and guidance skills in the voluntary, statutory or private sectors. Further details on CETAD can be found in Useful Addresses on page 187.

Thinking Slot 17

◆ From your list of activities with structured voluntary organisations, is there a similarity of roles you play in each one – or are they completely different? What do you think this tells you about your abilities?

Personal community work

In this category we are looking at the voluntary work you do perhaps without recognising it for what it is. This covers the non-structured activities you do for people who are not your relatives. It might be a regular or occasional commitment, such as the weekly shopping trip for a disabled neighbour; offering a lift to someone without transport to attend a hospital appointment or to visit a sick relative; or just popping in every morning to check an elderly person is all right. Other possibilities are reading newspapers for someone who is blind, or writing letters; taking or making phone calls for someone profoundly deaf; cutting a lawn every week for someone too frail to do this job anymore; feeding a dog or cat while its owner is in hospital and so on.

Your level of commitment to this type of voluntary community work may be a little, or it may be quite considerable. But regardless of the amount of time you give, because there is no organisational structure, the efficacy of what you do relies on your ability to maintain the expectations of those who depend on you.

Record your personal community work on Worksheet 23 (page 101). As with your record of leisure pursuits with other people, you may find it useful to note the time spent on the activity in hours per day, per week or per month.

Skills from your personal community work

Because the range of skills under this heading will depend on the activity, it is not possible to give an exhaustive list, but by now you will be aware of what these are likely to be from the previous

Worksheet 23: Personal community work

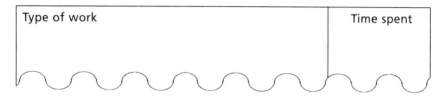

Type of work	Time spent

exercises you have carried out during the course of this book.

You will almost certainly expect to find some caring skills, not necessarily those associated with very personal services, but at least those involving the ability to sympathise and treat others in a caring and supportive manner. In some circumstances, your caring skills may include the nurturing and tending of plants or animals as well.

If you are involved in making meals, then you would obviously have cooking skills and possibly nutritional skills as well if you did the shopping. It is easy to forget that driving is a skill, but it is, so you should not forget to include it, as well as recording what type of vehicle you are licensed to drive.

Look at what you do and think of each activity in terms of what skills you need to do it.

Thinking Slot 18

♦ Looking at your list of community work, is there a common theme running through the activities which tends to show a preference in the type of activity you do?

Tackling your pastimes skills audit

As mentioned at the start of this chapter, your pastime skills are the last set of planks to add to your life raft. At this stage you will need very little help in picking out skills from the activity worksheets. Using Worksheet 24 (page 102), keep to the rule of one sheet per activity, with a fresh sheet for any positions you held (official or unofficial in this case) to identify the skills needed for these, as distinct from those arising from taking part in the activity itself. As previously, you should also try to provide evidence of your achievements or involvement where possible. Such evidence might be prizes, cups, medals, certificates, letters of appreciation and, of course, press cuttings and photographs.

Pastime activities, like school activities, are often the subject of

Worksheet 24: Pastime skills audit

Pastime:

Date (or length of involvement):

The pastime involved:

The skills I used were:

What I achieved:

Evidence of achievement or involvement:

What satisfaction does this pastime give me?

local newspaper reports. Many local papers could not survive if they did not have a policy of reporting the events of local groups: the jumble sales and coffee mornings; the bungee jumping and other whacky fund-raising events; formal dinners and annual general meetings; famous guest speakers and visiting patrons; or the presentation of awards.

Just like the collection of cuttings from your schooldays, any press cuttings you may have kept recording your involvement in this group or that may well be stuffed unceremoniously in the back of a chest of drawers. Now is the time to rescue them and keep them in a more orderly fashion in your clear plastic multipunched pockets as a permanent record in your PRP. If over the years you have not bothered to keep clippings, now is a good time to start – even if some of the photographs are ones you might prefer to suppress. The reason for keeping them is obvious – they are tangible evidence of your achievements or involvement. Incidentally, when you collect press cuttings do remember to date them – in years to come, when you might want to refer back to the time you were the secretary of the local angling club, this may be the only confirmation you have.

The last section of the audit worksheet is new: it asks you to think about *why* you have been doing what you do in your spare time. This is to set you thinking about what motivates you to get involved, not just in the pastime itself, but also in any additional role you have taken on, particularly in group situations.

Your motivation is important because this will help you see

which situations are the best for you no matter where you are in your life, or what you see as being your next stage. Knowing what you enjoy and what you can bring to a situation gives you a head start in your search for a more satisfying lifestyle.

Finally, extract all the skills you have identified using their broad category headings and list them under your 'Pastime skills' on the sheet set up at the start of this chapter.

Summary

Chapter 5 explored the skills you use in your spare time occupations.

◆ To help you identify these skills the distinction was made between *hobbies, leisure pursuits* and *voluntary work.*

◆ You were shown the distinction between formal and informal groups for the purposes of identifying different skills.

◆ By recognising the existence of an organisational structure you were able to appreciate the presence of skills additional to those needed in taking part in the activity itself.

◆ Your attention was drawn to the difference between physically active skills and the more passive types.

◆ You were encouraged to recognise the distinction between group activities and solitary pastimes, particularly in relation to how this affected your skills base.

◆ You were advised on which category certain types of activity should be allocated where the distinction was blurred.

◆ You were also introduced to the concept of transferring pastime skills into other activities, with particular reference to paid employment.

◆ Through Thinking Slots you were asked to start putting your skills into broad categories so you could begin to see any trends running through your pastimes.

◆ You were also asked to see if you had chosen a similar role in structured organisations to help identify personal preferences.

◆ As part of your pastimes audit you were encouraged to keep press cuttings and other evidence of your involvement in spare time activities as part of your PRP.

*My idea of good
company, Mr
Elliot, is the
company of clever,
well-informed
people...*
AUSTEN: PERSUASION

CHAPTER 6

Evaluating Social Skills

Social skills are crucially important to everyone. Unless you are keen to be a hermit or recluse, getting on with your fellow human beings, even if this is on the most mundane level, is one of the basic life skills you need to possess. The aim of this chapter is to get you thinking about your social skills and your ability to use them in a variety of situations.

But first it is necessary to review what you have been doing so far. Up until now we have been exploring the past. The journey has travelled forward from schooldays into experiences of work, home and spare time. From these explorations you should have been able to put together a dossier of facts – the activities which have shaped your life. These in turn have provided the basis for the skills audits which searched out the skills involved.

At the start of this book, life skills were described as the planks which made up a life raft to keep you afloat regardless of where you were on the sea of life. The skills audits should be thought of as these planks – the raw material from which the raft is made. From this chapter onwards, you will be thinking about ways in which to construct your raft to a design which is right for you. There is no standard pattern to follow simply because no two people have the same inputs into their lives, the same pressures or the same circumstances.

> Keep reminding yourself of your life skills.

How you design your own life raft will depend on how much work you have put into fashioning your planks, i.e. your skills audits. These audits from now on will be the main focus of attention. Because of this, if you were not entirely wholehearted in the process of extracting your skills and recording them in the various audits, you may not have as clear a picture to work from as you might have had. It might be useful at this stage to reread what you have recorded in your audits. Familiarising yourself in this way will help you pick out items more quickly, and would be particularly useful if you have been completing your audits over several weeks and have already forgotten some of the earlier entries.

Thinking Slot 19

◆ Are your skills audits complete enough to be used as valid resource documents?

◆ If not, what do you intend to do to rectify the situation?

Setting up your cross-reference audits

So far your skills audits have been drawn from different aspects of your life. The next task is to extract from these audits specific skills of a similar type and the circumstances which illustrate when, where and how you used them. In the case of this chapter we will be looking for social skills.

To help you compile this cross-reference audit, a worksheet layout is suggested on page 120, but before filling in any details you will need to think about the types of categories you want to use.

You will see that you also need to record when you used the skill in question to remind yourself whether this is an old skill, now long out of regular use, or one which is still being exercised. You will also need space to record any thoughts you may have about whether there are any skills showing particular strengths or weaknesses, and in the case of the second group, whether you would like to work on improving these – and how this might be achieved.

In the following sections we will be looking at some old friends, categories of skills already met and discussed in part. Here they are to be looked at in the specific context of social, or interpersonal situations, where how you get on with people matters in terms of the outcome.

No one, with the exception of a masochist perhaps, engages in a social exchange with the aim of being made to feel inferior, or to be the subject of a tirade of abuse. Interpersonal chemistry, however, does not always work, and you will inevitably meet occasions when the person or persons around you are intent on forcing their opinions on you whether you like it or not. Equally, you may find yourself in the position of having to 'force' your opinion on someone else. Anyone working in a supervisory capacity has at some stage to draw a line with a subordinate who is not performing well enough. Any parent with a teenager around the home will have experienced a similar situation.

Social skills are all about achieving the goal you are aiming for to the satisfaction, or relative satisfaction, of everyone, while at the same time recognising there are occasions when this will not be possible. The hope must always be that such occasions will be the exception rather than the rule.

Communicating and listening

Under this heading we will be looking at:

◆ verbal language
◆ written language
◆ signalling
◆ body language
◆ constructive listening
◆ evaluating information
◆ providing feedback.

With the exception of *written language* and *signalling* all the above subject headings are part of everyday conversations. But to be really effective, conversation demands a good quality of interaction between the contributors – and you can't always guarantee this component. However, you can always try to make sure that *your* contribution is up to scratch.

Verbal language

> Good communication skills add up to saying what you mean and meaning what you say.

To do this you have to

◆ be clear about your message;
◆ choose the right vocabulary;
◆ choose the right tone of voice;
◆ speak clearly.

Being clear about your message

Before you can get your message across, you have to be
thoroughly confident you know precisely what you are trying to
say. Woolly thinking inevitably produces woolly words. The result
– your listener receives a confused message. Confused messages
leave interpretation to the listener who may or may not get it
right. This is useful to those who intentionally want to let
individual listeners choose what they want to hear, but actions
based on misinterpretations can be not only misdirected but in
some cases potentially dangerous.

Choosing the right vocabulary

No one would try to use the same level of vocabulary when
talking to a young child socially as they would to a group of
colleagues. Good communication relies on picking the right sort
of vocabulary to match the understanding of your listeners or
audience. Almost everyone has a different 'set' of words or phrases
which they use to meet different situations. The 'set' used in the
home will include 'in-house' words, phrases or sayings which to
an outsider might be totally incomprehensible. Peer groups
develop their own vocabulary only understood by those who are
part of the group. Work-based jargon has the same function. We
all of us carry around with us several 'sets' from which we pick the
one which is most appropriate at the time. Pick the wrong one,
and your listeners will simply not hear you.

Choosing the right tone of voice

> You will muddle your message if you deliver it using a tone of
> voice which does not match what you are saying.

For instance, if you are trying to be encouraging but sound harsh,
or even angry, the anger will come across more strongly than the
words you are using. Equally, if your attempts to bring someone
up short are delivered in muted tones, you are diluting the force of
what you are trying to say.

Speaking clearly

It should go without saying that you cannot hope to get your
message across if you do not deliver your words clearly

pronounced and at a pitch which makes it possible for them to be heard. This includes adapting your volume to match the space you are talking in: conversational tones will simply get lost in a hall and, conversely, there is no need to bellow in a confined area.

Written language

Written language skill means being clear about what you want to convey and writing it in a way that can easily be understood. The principles are similar to verbal language guidelines. It's all about

- knowing what you want to say;
- adapting your writing style to the recipient;
- writing clearly.

Knowing what you want to say

Written communication can be generated by yourself to raise queries or comment on events, or by other people who expect you to reply to their queries or comments. To be effective in what you write, you need to be able to identify the core points to be included in the report, letter or whatever, and your reaction to these. Written waffle can be as confusing as verbal waffle – with roughly the same effects.

Adapting your writing style to the recipient

This is the same approach as adopting the right verbal vocabulary to match the understanding of your listener. You would adopt a more formal style of prose in an official letter or report than you would if you were writing to a friend. You would also perhaps use words you would not normally use in everyday speech to give added meaning or emphasis to what you are writing. Writing style therefore combines both the right vocabulary for the occasion and the choice of words to reinforce the meaning which would otherwise come across in your tone of voice if you were speaking.

Writing clearly

Rather obviously, writing clearly is essential. Illegible handwriting obscures the message in the same way as indistinct speech. If you are not blessed with a clear script, you will either have to develop one or use a typewriter or word processor – which demand other skills.

Signalling

Signalling skills are specialist skills, such as the use of:

◆ sign language
◆ finger spelling
◆ Braille
◆ semaphore
◆ Morse
◆ other codes.

All these means of getting the message across require a detailed knowledge of a different type of language, its structure and the means of delivery. Most use the hands to a greater or lesser extent, although some newer forms of communication for the severely disabled operate by eye movement alone.

The level of skills under this heading are sophisticated and should never be undervalued.

Body language

Much of our body language is subconscious and for that reason it is difficult to hide our inner emotions or intentions from others. However, some body language can consciously be worked on to help improve communication skills. The most important are:

◆ eye contact
◆ gestures.

Using eye contact

Eye contact is an important feature of conversation both for the speaker and the listener. If either party is gazing around while speaking or listening, they are either not paying attention or have some other reason for not engaging in the process. The result is always the same – poor communication and often a sense of irritation in the unfortunate person on the receiving end of this behaviour.

Eye contact does not mean staring at someone, which could seem intimidating, illustrating the phrase 'brazening it out'. Good eye contact is the art of being able to talk or listen while looking at the area bounded by the other person's eyes, nose and mouth, with occasional brief glances away during periods of thought. Long breaks between eye contact by a speaker can often indicate lack of confidence, indecision, or even lying. Just watch politicians in an unrehearsed situation. Good eye contact by a listener indicates interest in what is being said; poor contact usually means lack of interest, or worse, boredom.

You can always improve the positive effects of eye contact by using the 'smiling eyes' approach when handling situations where you want to shine but feel at a disadvantage in some way.

Using positive gestures

Unless you are cold or have a stomach ache, the 'arms folded in front of you' pose gives a strong negative message to someone communicating with you. It suggests a defensive attitude, either hugging yourself for protection or putting up a barrier between yourself and someone else because you disagree with them. If you can avoid folding your arms during a discussion you want to keep open and productive, you are less likely to set off negative response patterns from the other party.

Constructive listening

Constructive listening involves letting the other person finish what they are saying and not butting in. It is very easy when you are animated to have your head full of thoughts you want to express. At this point you are not really listening to *the other person*, you are concentrating on what *you* want to say. If both parties behave in this way the conversation gets nowhere because it becomes a series of statements by both parties and no exchange of ideas, thoughts or opinions takes place. The art lies in listening and framing your reply based on what you have heard, which leads on to the next topic.

Evaluating information

Part of the process of constructive listening is evaluating the information you are getting from the speaker, analysing the content, drawing conclusions from your analysis, and deciding how to respond. Your response may be verbal, or if you feel this would be unhelpful under the circumstances, particularly in volatile situations, you may decide to keep silent. Silence can often speak volumes.

Providing feedback

Feedback is the verbal reaction to what you have heard and how you have decided to respond to it. A speaker may expect a particular form of response because the attitude, tone of voice and vocabulary used have given strong pointers as to what is wanted. How you respond will depend on how well you have been listening, how you feel about what you have heard and whether you feel any verbal response is either useful or necessary. By framing your reply in a different manner from the speaker to encourage a different reaction, you can either calm a potentially difficult situation or bring it to the boil.

Interacting and coordinating

How we respond in a social setting can often depend on the number of people involved and the reason for the social exchange taking place. As examples, we will be looking at:

◆ one-to-one discussions
◆ group dynamics
◆ linking action to team members.

One-to-one discussions

We all respond to people differently in different circumstances, and the more people there are in a group, the greater the variation in our responses.

The tête-à-tête is very intense because there are only two people involved with no one else to interpose. It can range from being a cosy, intimate chat between friends to a full-blown row, or a formal interview conducted with polite conversation to a dressing down with no holds barred. The verbal language used is everything and our personal command of it can be a help or a hindrance. So, too, can the interpersonal chemistry which exists between the two parties and the individual status, perceived or actual, which can affect response patterns. Knowing how to handle a dialogue in all its many forms, and the ability to alter your response to different demands can be a huge advantage in coping with some of the more stressful situations you are likely to meet throughout life.

Group dynamics

As soon as there are more than two people in a social setting, a whole set of variables starts to creep into the interaction taking place. The intensity of the one-to-one format has gone so that a relaxed group with no peer pressures will form a comfortable homogeneous mix of equals.

However, there are occasions when even with a group of three, two members begin to join forces against the third, isolating this individual and making their contribution less important. In a much larger group, isolating someone is very threatening to the person concerned and a very destructive form of group dynamics: it will almost inevitably lead to the removal of that person from the group either because they voluntarily choose to leave, or because group pressure forces them to go.

Larger groups will almost always split into factions. This can have a positive or negative effect: positive in that it is sometimes essential for two or more sets of ideas to circulate freely in order for the best to be chosen; negative if there is no interchange of ideas but a polarisation which ultimately fractures the group. It all comes down to how the group is constituted and the attitudes individuals bring with them to the group.

Individual attitudes undergo subtle changes in different groups: sometimes being prepared to be led by others; sometimes doing the leading.

> It is not uncommon for individuals to behave entirely 'out of character' in circumstances where they feel obliged, or threatened by peer pressure to act in a particular way.

Linking action to team members

Coordinating activities takes place in group situations. The art of coordinating lies in making sure that those who are taking part in the exercise understand what the goal is, how it is to be achieved, and who is responsible for which part of the process to get there.

To be part of a coordination process, you need to feel confident the best person for the job of coordinator is doing the job. And to be confident, you need to know the strengths and weaknesses of the personalities involved, not necessarily with them ever being aware that this evaluation is taking place. You can only truly know about people's strengths and weaknesses by observing them, weighing up how they have responded in the past and evaluating how you believe they will achieve in the future.

Coordinating a group you have never met before means you have to take short cuts to get the answers you want. Often the only way of doing this is by asking for volunteers or encouraging people to show they have the necessary skills to apply themselves to the task. So good communication skills are vital to get your message across effectively. You will also need to demonstrate the self-confidence to be accepted by the other members of the group in the coordinating role.

Negotiating and holding your own

Part of group dynamics is your contribution to the way a group functions and the way you handle yourself as the process takes place. In this section we will be looking at:

◆ helping others to agree, make decisions or act
◆ being assertive.

Although we are looking at these aspects separately, they can be interrelated in some situations. This is particularly true where in order to facilitate the negotiation procedure, you have to state your viewpoint in such a way that everyone recognises you wish your very firm opinion to be noted.

Helping others to agree, make decisions or act

Negotiations are not just the well-publicised wrangles between employers and employees over the annual pay award, or the release of hostages, they are part of our everyday lives: who will do what and when; which member of the household will do the washing up after breakfast, or which neighbour will collect the children from school.

Your role may be an adjunct to the process because you are not involved in the process itself. In this situation you are the facilitator – the person who acts as the go-between or sounding board between the different standpoints. In this role, you not only need good communication skills, you have to have the ability to withstand any flak which comes your way from disgruntled participants. You also need to be able to demonstrate you are even-handed in your approach.

If you are part of the negotiation process and there is no facilitator to put your case or to act as the buffer zone, you need not just good communication skills but a hefty slice of self-control.

> Negotiation isn't just about having your say, but persuading others that what you are saying makes good sense, is a reasonable course to follow, and is to the benefit of the majority.

Being assertive

This is *not* about being domineering or overpowering: it is all about putting across your point of view firmly so that your listener or audience understands this is how you feel and you want everyone to know precisely that. It is also about holding your own when there is pressure put on you to change your mind; about having the courage of your convictions. This is the sort of situation which can arise where you are a member of a jury and the only person to hold a contrary view to the rest.

If you have spent your life in subordinate roles where your opinion has never counted for a great deal, being assertive is a skill you may feel you lack. In the 1980s, when more women were beginning to return to work after having their family, it was recognised that once out of the home environment many women did not feel they had sufficient confidence to assert themselves in the workplace. At that time, a concerted effort was made to introduce assertiveness training as part of the process of helping women to return to work after their career breaks.

Encouraging and supporting

These two interrelated skills are important where you are not necessarily involved directly in the activities of someone who needs your help. These are counselling skills and the most obvious occasion when they are used is in the parental role, whether the topic is homework or boy/girlfriend trouble. We will look at:

- giving praise
- obtaining information to give advice
- offering guidance
- providing continuing help and support.

Giving praise

Giving praise is the ability to recognise what someone has achieved, evaluating it against previous performance and saying 'Well done' in a way which shows you have made an honest appraisal of the performance. Perfunctory praise, given without any attempt at the evaluation element, is not a skill, it is laziness, and the person on the receiving end can usually spot it a mile off.

Giving praise is an important part of the process of encouraging the development of good practice. In many circumstances, this feedback is probably almost as important as the achievement itself because it conveys a validity by someone else that you have performed to a satisfactory standard.

Obtaining information to give advice

You cannot give sound advice without first knowing more about the problem or the set of circumstances involved. This is a pure counselling skill and involves the ability to put questions to someone in a way which will elicit the right information to work on; in other words, asking 'open' questions: who? what? when? where? how? in a tactful and courteous manner.

This skill can be refined and adapted for other purposes, such as part of the formal interview process for recruitment or selection, or at the extreme end of the spectrum without any frills attached for the purposes of interrogation.

Offering guidance

This follows on from the last process. Once you have the information to work from, how you offer the guidance sought sometimes needs more delicate handling than eliciting the information itself: the advice is not always what the listener wants to hear.

To be successful, your interpersonal skills have to work overtime. You need to be able to judge the state of mind of the person you are advising; to evaluate the effect your advice will have under those circumstances, and be able to couch your words in terms which will make it possible for the guidance to be acceptable, even if unpalatable.

One thing is certain:

> If you deliver your guidance in a pompous or arrogant manner, it will he ignored, however valid it might be.

Providing continuing help and support

One-off counselling may be sufficient in some cases, but there are other situations where it needs to be more long term. Giving long-term support within the family is relatively easy, firstly because you know the personalities involved, and secondly, because the difficulties or problems are likely to be in front of you on a day-to-day basis and you are having constant updates on the situation.

Where you are providing longer-term support in other scenarios, however, say at work or for a friend, you need additional skills: the ability to recall the finer nuances and facts from earlier discussions; to be able to absorb fresh information, and to pitch your responses at exactly the same level as previously.

Enabling and advising

These skills are linked to *encouraging and supporting* but in situations where you are actively helping people involved in similar activities to your own. They are skills usually linked to supervisory roles in the workplace, and used to encourage personal development or to expand an employee's capabilities as part of a training programme.

We will look at these skills under the headings:

◆ empowering
◆ mentoring.

Empowering

Empowerment is a business concept of the 1990s and is a management skill. It arose from the remorseless restructuring of organisations which thinned out several layers of middle management and expected greater flexibility from the workforce in the range and type of jobs they would do.

What empowerment does is to allow individuals or groups the power, opportunity and the means to think and act for themselves within the framework of the aims of a team or organisation.

Consequently, empowering people involves a less rigid approach to management and the softening of the edges of status and power. There is less directing and more interchanging of ideas which respect the individual's ability to contribute constructively to problem-solving.

Someone who cannot free themselves from a more authoritarian model of managing people will find the skills needed to adopt this type of approach very difficult to master.

Mentoring

In the workplace this used to be known as 'sitting next to Nellie'. Trainees would sit next to experienced employees and watch what they did. Gradually, they would take part in the process themselves until they were skilled enough to do the job unsupervised.

In its more modern reincarnation mentoring is a mixture of advising and guiding using a light touch to direct and encourage while providing a backstop where needed. You need all the interpersonal skills involved in *encouraging and supporting* put into the context of the organisational framework.

Leading and directing

These skills are rather obviously leadership skills, although they can be thought of as being the two sides of the same coin. Under *leadership* we will consider:

◆ taking the initiative
◆ inspiring confidence in others
◆ taking responsibility
◆ caring about others.

Under *directing* we will look at:

◆ giving orders
◆ taking responsibility for your actions.

Leadership as an interpersonal skill

A good leader is part of the action, up there at the front – leading.

Leaders only exist because other people have allowed them to lead, either through formal selection or informal agreement: there is a common perception that they are the best choice for the task in hand. Leadership is not about being a dictator: it is being the first among equals. Your performance is under constant review by your followers and if you do not perform as expected, you not only lose your position but in all probability you will lose face as well.

Taking the initiative

In any group, the leader is expected to take the initiative, to come up with answers and take any action necessary. A leader has to have persuasive powers to encourage followers that, however reluctant they might be, the proposed course of action is the best way forward. To prove it, you will be expected to plunge into the task along with everyone else.

Inspiring confidence in others

Actions may speak louder than words, and being ahead of the rest is undoubtedly a spur to others, but the bottom line is all about confidence building. If you have failed to persuade others of the strength of your argument, you can find yourself the leader of one – yourself. Everyone else has let you get on with it and is standing back not participating. You may prove your point by achieving what you set out to do, but you have not taken everyone with you. An isolated leader has effectively ceased to be a leader.

Taking responsibility

No leader can duck responsibility for what happens as a result of their leadership, and more importantly for what happens to those who followed their lead. If something goes wrong as a result of your leadership, you must be prepared not only to take the criticism, but to apologise to those who were persuaded to follow you. Both these situations demand a high level of personal resilience, an ability to admit to an error of judgement, and the humility to accept censure.

Caring about others

Caring skills are not usually much associated with leadership, but to be a good leader you must care about the people who invest themselves in your leadership and give you their support. There is obviously an element of self-interest here in nurturing your followers because by doing so you reinforce your position as their leader. But superficial caring is not enough: you really must *care* and have an empathy with your group, or committee, or whatever, because this quality can have a powerful binding force which strengthens the team spirit.

Directing as an interpersonal skill

> Not everyone can be a leader in the mould of Alexander the Great.

Directing people, or in the more extreme form, dictating to them, is found more frequently than the pure form of leadership. The difference between being a leader and a director is that most directors are rarely up front as part of the action: they are too busy telling other people what to do from a distance.

Not every set of circumstances in a social context can be resolved by leadership. In any setting where a hierarchy exists, whether this is the parental hierarchy of the home, the teacher at school, or the boss at work, the guidance given is by direction and not by example and involves a very different set of skills.

Giving orders

How you give orders is as important as the orders themselves. Verbal orders need a good command of the spoken word; written orders a good command of the written word. As with all communication without visual example for people to follow, an order must be clear and precise, otherwise it will be open to misinterpretation.

Giving orders also requires positive interpersonal chemistry between yourself and the people you are giving the orders to. Treating people in an inappropriate manner will only produce grudging compliance at best and open hostility at worst. Orders will only be acceptable, too, if the way they are delivered matches the environment they are delivered in. No one outside the armed services would be prepared to follow orders given in the manner of the parade ground. You need the skill to be able to pitch your directions at the right level if you are to achieve the result you want.

Taking responsibility for your actions

As a director, taking responsibility for your actions is probably more difficult to handle than if you were acting as a leader of equals. People have followed your orders because they had no alternative and, as subordinates, were in no position to affect your decision. Even if they were able to argue against a particular course of action, you could override their reservations. So if you make a gaffe, you will not have the same intense loyalty to give you moral, if not actual, support. There is no collective sense of failure, just your own.

You need to be a very strong personality to feel confident you can manage the pressures of having a directing role and the ability to deflect negative criticism into a positive learning experience.

Completing your social skills audit

It is now time to complete the first of your cross-reference audits. To do this you will need to have Worksheets 9, 10, 13, 16 and 24 to work from. Start by rereading these and drawing out your social skills. List these on a separate sheet headed 'Social skills', then take each skill in turn and complete a Worksheet 25 for each of them. If you have one or several social skills which are being used more often than others, highlight these by making a separate list to draw attention to them.

Worksheet 25: Social skills audit

Category of skill:

Instances of use and dates:

My strengths are:

My weaknesses are:

Areas I would like to improve:

I could improve these skills by:

What have you discovered?

Your social skills audit should have provided you with a good indication of which skills you use most and to what level. This should give you confidence to use these skills in different circumstances, or to decide to upgrade your competence in them, and how you could achieve this improvement. Practice inevitably helps, but sometimes additional input from an external source, whether this comes from a specific formal training programme or useful feedback by a trusted friend, can be useful.

As we discussed at the start of this chapter, we all need social skills to smooth our paths on a day-to-day basis because few of us can, or would want to avoid human contact altogether.

Summary

This chapter concentrated on social skills as part of your life skills raft.

+ You began by reviewing your skills audits to ensure they were detailed enough to be used as reference documents from which to extract your social skills.
+ You began to think about social skills and their crucial importance to everyday life.
+ You extracted social skills from your educational, pastime, occupational and home-based skills audits and considered your strengths and weaknesses.
+ You were encouraged to think of these skills as invaluable and worthy of improvement or development.

CHAPTER 7

Recognising Portable Skills

I n this chapter the aim will be to help anyone who feels somehow trapped in a lifestyle which is no longer for them and unable to see any way of escaping from it.

One of the problems of feeling in any way trapped by circumstances beyond our control is the accompanying sense of powerlessness; of thinking there is no way out, or of not being able to see any alternative. This sense of being stifled can often result from blinkered vision: of looking at life from a narrowly focused perspective. To find an escape route all you need is the ability to remove the blinkers. Often, the key to this is to stop putting up self-made barriers.

Lack of self-confidence is probably the main obstacle builder: 'I can't do that at my age', 'I've no experience', or any other negative reason you may put forward to explain your predicament should not be allowed to pass without serious examination. There are times when such statements are made as a way of saying you don't *want* to do something. But this is very different from saying you don't believe you have what it takes.

Portable skills

Several times already in earlier chapters we have touched on how skills in one area can be transferred into others. Transferable skills, or portable skills as they are now more commonly known, are your greatest strengths. They offer you the opportunity to use a particular talent in a different way to achieve different ends at different times in your life. They are, if you like, the most important planks in your life raft.

Everyone's life is filled with a huge variety of experiences and abilities which are completely unique to that person alone. Consequently it is impossible to give prescriptive guidance that will suit everyone's needs or circumstances. That challenge has to be met by the individual.

As you did in Chapter 6, you will need to refer to your skills audits on Worksheets 9, 10, 13, 16 and 24. The task will be to search out the skills you have been using most frequently in the four main areas of your life – school, home, spare time and work – to see if there are any skills you have already been transferring from one sector to another, perhaps without realising. At the same time, you will be looking at every skill and asking yourself whether each ability can be transferred into other situations, and if so, which ones.

As a way of helping you to think about opportunities to develop your own life, over this and the remaining chapters we will be using case studies as a basis for discussion. But to begin with we will go back to the educational skills you identified from Chapter 2.

Using educational skills as pointers

You will remember in Chapter 2 we looked at the range of skills you were likely to have encountered during your time in a formal educational environment. These included:

- core skills (literacy, numeracy and communication)
- computer literacy
- language skills
- technical skills
- analysis and evaluation skills
- time management skills
- leadership skills
- team working
- skills from individual self-expression
- interpersonal skills.

Some or all of these skills will have been included in your educational skills audits (Worksheets 9 and 10).

Your use of these skills while at school or college will not have been to any great depth: these are your 'green' or immature skills. But that does not make them any the less important. Instead of discounting them you should look on them as pointers, as a way of possibly confirming later trends. Many of our later decisions in life have their roots in what we did or chose not to do as part of our extra-curricular activities.

At this stage you need to compare the skills you identified in your educational skills audits (Worksheets 9 and 10) with those in your home-based skills (Worksheet 16), pastime skills (Worksheet 24) and occupational skills (Worksheet 13) audits and pick out those skills you have transported with you out of the world of education and into the rest of your life.

As you begin to spot these portable skills you will also start to see how they have been adapted and used in new contexts. For instance, your membership of a school club or team may have developed into membership of another type of club or team in later years. It may be that the focus of the group is the same, but even if it is different, you are still gravitating towards the group rather than enjoying more solitary activities. In other words, you enjoy being part of a team and your skills will be those associated with teamworking.

Similarly you may have been responsible for organising a charity event for your fellow students and later in life have taken on the role of fund-raiser with a community organisation. In this situation, although you are working as part of a team, you have opted for a particular role which reflects the earlier choice you made and the skills which were needed to carry it out effectively.

Adapting home-based skills

The importance of home-based skills has been repeatedly emphasised because these skills still remain largely undervalued or even unrecognised. This has been very much the case in the past where the responsibility of bringing up children or looking after ageing parents has fallen predominantly on women. But it should not be forgotten that there are thousands of children as well as adults in the UK who regularly undertake the responsibilities of the caring role.

There is nothing new about children taking the place of an ailing parent in running a household, often looking after younger siblings as well. Was this your responsibility when you were young?

If you were in this position yourself as a child, have you included in your home-based skills audit all the jobs you did in this role and extracted the skills you needed to complete your tasks successfully? Even if you were not a carer, there may have been tasks which were allocated specifically for you to complete, such as cleaning out the rabbits, walking the dog, digging the vegetable patch, doing the washing or ironing, and so on. Just because you were a child does not diminish the importance of your skill, even if you were reluctant to carry out the duties involved.

Someone who has been living the restricted lifestyle of a carer for many years can feel totally at a loss when the role of carer comes to an end. Very often someone in this situation is mentally and physically exhausted and needs time and space to pick themselves up. But how to fill the void left in their lives can seem an impossible task. At this point we will look at an example of how recognising the skills you have can help you put some life back into your life.

Case study: Ruth _____

Ruth Harris is now 48 years old and unmarried. She did well at her high school (Maurice Lattimer in Railsford) where she was popular and in demand. She was captain of the school hockey team and was particularly good at French. She joined the school's French Society which travelled to France every summer holiday and completed her sixth form studies with exceptionally high marks in her A Level exam.

From school Ruth went to University and then Teacher Training College, returning to Maurice Lattimer as a French teacher and becoming Head of Department four years later. As Head of Department she resurrected the French Society which had not been running for five years and organised trips to France on a biannual basis to meet demand.

Ruth had been running the Department for six years when her widowed mother suffered a major stroke. Feeling unable to 'abandon' her, as she saw it, to someone else's care, Ruth gave up her job and became a full-time carer for the next 14 years. Her mother has just died and Ruth is now having to face the challenge of rebuilding her own life.

Like other carers in her position, Ruth is physically and mentally weary. She has lost contact with all her friends and colleagues over the years and has no interest in trying to return to teaching which seems to her a radically different type of job to the one she left. Added to this, she has dropped all her earlier pastimes which included tennis and organising trips to musical concerts with colleagues, and her linguistic skills have been dulled by lack of regular use, although she has managed to keep in touch with a penfriend in

France. She badly wants to build up a social life again. Although she is not short of money, she is not well-off either, and is toying with the idea of looking for a job to get her out of the house and back into a more socially-orientated lifestyle. Her main stumbling block, however, is her loss of self-confidence through limited contacts outside the home. _____

Ruth's skills base

Ruth's broad range of skills can be summed up as follows:

Educational:	◆ high level of competence in French;
	◆ good team worker (hockey team);
	◆ good leadership skills (captain of the team);
	◆ social skills as part of the French Society.
Pastime:	◆ high level of competence in French;
	◆ good hand/eye coordination in tennis;
	◆ social skills as part of the tennis club;
	◆ good team player in doubles matches;
	◆ good organisational skills (arranging concert trips).
Occupational:	◆ high level of competence in French;
	◆ good communication and instruction skills (teacher);
	◆ wide range of management skills (Head of Department);
	◆ good organisational skills (arranging school trips).
Home-based:	◆ good home maintenance skills;
	◆ excellent household management skills (organisational);
	◆ excellent caring and supporting skills.

If you look through these skills there are several portable skills showing up as trends as Ruth uses them in different situations. These are:

◆ linguistic abilities
◆ communicating
◆ teamworking
◆ organising
◆ leading
◆ instructing

- managing
- maintaining.

What is also important from Ruth's point of view is that these skills are predominantly associated with group activities rather than solitary ones, which is why the last 14 years have left her so mentally exhausted and unstimulated.

Options for Ruth

Ruth needs to build up her self-confidence again as a first step to broadening her horizons and getting herself back into a more socially focused environment.

Although she has exhausted her interest in caring, during the 14 years devoted to her mother she has gained a wealth of experience about the problems a carer has to face and the areas where support is most needed. As a teacher she is used to communicating with other people and offering advice and guidance, even though this skill has been lying dormant for several years. Giving other carers the benefit of her experience or the opportunity to share their own experiences with her could provide a way of widening her circle of acquaintances. Counselling initially in a one-to-one situation could be the basis of revitalising her teaching skills, allowing her time to readjust to talking to groups of 20 or 30 people. Offering her skills to the local social services department or carer support group on a voluntary basis would not only open up a wider circle of contacts but also allow her the chance to hone up those skills she has not had the opportunity to use for some time.

Another option, which might have to wait until Ruth has regained some of her self-confidence, is the possibility of using her teaching skills in a different setting, i.e. by providing private tuition in French. In this way, she would be getting back into the world of work on her own terms without the pressures she feels she could no longer cope with. Taking this one step further, as she no longer has any ties in the UK, she could use the long-standing contact with her French penfriend to live and work in France for a while to refresh the range of her linguistic skills. Once she was confidently established there, it would be a natural progression to consider tutoring French students wanting to learn English.

How Ruth can progress

From what appears at first glance to be a forlorn future for someone in Ruth's position, you can see an array of interesting opportunities opening up. Each move acts as a stepping stone to the next. Building on current skills revitalises older skills, while older skills provide access to additional skills.

Putting pastime skills to other uses

In Chapter 5 we explored your pastime skills in detail, drawing out the different types of pastimes, i.e.:

- hobbies
- leisure pursuits and
- voluntary work

and considering the significance of these differences.

From the point of view of portable skills, your pastime skills are extremely valuable because, as you may remember, what you do in your spare time is what you *want* to do, not what you *have* to do. As a result, all the skills which come from your spare-time pursuits are either those which could be described as 'natural abilities', or are the result of your willingness to acquire them.

From the work you did in producing your pastime skills audit (Worksheet 24), you should have a sound basis for extracting those skills which run through your spare-time activities. They are likely to be a mixture of the following broad categories:

- dexterity or good physical coordination abilities
- rapid reaction abilities
- use of subject knowledge
- understanding or carrying out rules or instructions
- time management and scheduling
- creating or performing
- caring or tending
- administrative abilities
- financial handling abilities
- teamworking
- individual motivation
- communication skills

- leadership skills
- organising and coordinating skills
- social and interpersonal skills.

Although most of your portable skills from spare-time pursuits are likely to have the greatest impact in the employment environment, they can still affect your home-based skills as well. For instance, your improved communication skills as a club committee member may have given you confidence in talking to social workers about the needs of your elderly father, or enabled you to feel more at ease coping with discussions on your children's progress at school on parents' evenings. Becoming a qualified first-aider has meant you are much more competent to deal with accidents within the home, or by giving your time as an adult literacy tutor you have acquired the skill to help your children to read and write more competently.

But undoubtedly the primary strength of pastime skills is their ability to be transferred into the world of work, which makes them very portable indeed. This aspect will be looked at in more detail in Chapter 8 where they will be directly linked to the types of skills which are regularly sought by employers in their job advertisements.

Seeing occupational skills as multi-purpose abilities

There is a tendency to think of the skills we use at work as being relevant only in the context of the workplace: portable only in the sense that they can be transferred from one job to the next, either as a specialist skill or one which can be adapted to suit a new organisational structure, such as administrative or financial management skills.

> Work-based skills are capable of being transferred out of the work environment altogether to be used in completely different contexts.

Take basic administration skills for example: setting up systems, organising meetings, taking notes, writing letters, keeping files and updating records. These are all skills which can readily be absorbed into running any sort of formal organisation with an executive body at its head, whether this is a charitable trust or a local football team.

But it isn't just the spare-time interests which benefit. Household management requires similar skills so that bills get paid on time, the boiler gets its annual servicing contract renewed, and everyone's birth certificate is in the blue folder under 'C' for 'Certificates' in the family's record file.

The same can be true of house maintenance, where trade skills of a professional standard are part and parcel of the running of the home and the maintenance of its systems.

The way we work and the type of work we do often embeds itself in our lives without our noticing that we are replicating our work skills at home and at play. As you compare your skills in the workplace (Worksheet 13) to those in your other audits, you will start to see those which have been used as a direct result of your work experience, or which have strengthened existing skills in other areas.

Coming to terms with a crisis

Sometimes our lives can be changed in a moment: we go from total certainty, to total uncertainty. In situations like these, portable skills really can become a life raft: something we can hang on to to keep us afloat. In the next case study we see an example where someone's life is turned upside down, not from an external event as in Ruth's case, but through a personal accident.

Case study: Louise

Louise Shaw is 25 years old, the youngest of four daughters. A very bubbly, sociable, good-looking girl from a well-heeled country background, she enjoyed riding from early childhood, a hobby that came naturally because her parents ran a riding stable. Educated at a private boarding school with a heavy emphasis on turning out very articulate students, she graduated in English and took additional secretarial qualifications with the aim of becoming a personal assistant. Within a few months of gaining her qualifications she achieved her goal, becoming PA to the Branch Manager of the Winchampton office of Railsford Estates, the long-established auctioneers, valuers and estate agents. Here, her persuasive selling techniques combined with polished personal presentational skills made her a highly valued employee. She became interested in antiques and works of art and was being encouraged to think about studying ceramics as a specialism, something she was keen to do as she studied pottery at residential courses during the long summer school holidays.

Everything changed a year ago. Her horse stumbled while taking a jump during a cross-country event and both fell badly. Louise was trapped between her mount and the fence and suffered multiple fractures. She spent almost six months in hospital undergoing a series of operations but now cannot walk without crutches, has only partial use of her right hand and still has very noticeable facial scarring. She still needs several more months of regular physiotherapy to strengthen muscles which were out of use for a considerable length of time.

Louise's family have been very supportive and want to do anything they can to help but as yet she has not been able to come to terms with her new condition. She actively discouraged her friends from visiting her in hospital and consequently they have drifted away from her. This rift has been widened because they were a close knit group which travelled to regular riding events and, although Louise knows she will be able to ride again at some stage in the future, it will not be the sort of riding her friends would be interested in.

Her difficulties are also increased because she feels unable to relate to anyone outside the family who knew her before the accident. Consequently, she has also resigned from her job at Railsford Estates, even though they had not filled her post during her stay in hospital and were keen to find a way of keeping her services.

Louise is now locked into a restricted lifestyle which she knows is partially of her own making. She desperately wants to find a job to occupy her time and to stop her slipping into hopelessness, but at the moment she cannot see any way forward, particularly as she is still so very self-conscious about her disfigurement and disability. _____

Louise's skills base

Louise's skills are not as broad as Ruth's simply because she did not have sufficient time or opportunity to develop and extend her range before her accident. Nonetheless, they provide a starting point. They are:

Educational:
- ◆ excellent communication skills, both verbal and written;
- ◆ excellent social skills;
- ◆ excellent interpersonal skills;
- ◆ high level of secretarial competence and organising ability.

Pastime:
- ◆ good equestrian skills and ability to train horses and riders;
- ◆ good pottery skills;
- ◆ good hand/eye coordination for both pastimes.

Occupational:
- ◆ excellent communication skills, both verbal and written;
- ◆ excellent social skills;
- ◆ excellent interpersonal skills;
- ◆ high level of secretarial competence and organising ability;
- ◆ good hand/eye coordination on keyboard;
- ◆ foundation skills in identifying ceramics;
- ◆ foundation skills in valuation techniques.

Louise's skills base has been distorted by her accident so that some of her previous skills will be impossible to use *in their existing form*. For instance, she is unlikely to be able to ride competitively again, but her knowledge of training horses and riders remains in place. Similarly, the restricted movement of her hand means that she will not be able to carry on with her pottery, but her budding knowledge of ceramics will allow her to transfer a physical skill into a related knowledge-based skill. Her previously good level of hand/eye coordination has also suffered in relation to her keyboard skills, but this may be overcome by touch-screen and mouse-activated technology.

Louise's strongest areas are those associated with her high level of articulation and interpersonal skills and these are at present undermined by her self-consciousness and loss of self-confidence.

Options for Louise

Louise, like Ruth, has lost her self-confidence, but unlike Ruth has erected her own barriers in the way of making any progress. Until she is ready to remove them, all her skills will continue to lie dormant.

In situations like this, new skills begin to emerge to take account of the changed circumstances and the necessity of adapting to a new way of life. As part of her physiotherapy sessions Louise attends Railsford Hospital's physiotherapy department. These sessions take place with patients who are still in hospital, and just as others encouraged Louise when she first started learning to walk again, she is finding herself as involved in the progress of these new patients as she is in her own.

Although she very much wants to forget her time in hospital, the experience has expanded her understanding of an individual's struggle to regain some measure of independence and mobility. Being able to encourage someone else in their struggle is likely to be the start of the dismantling of some of her self-imposed barriers, particularly when the other person is wrestling with similar physical and emotional damage.

Encouraging others by example or by giving advice is a skill related to training, and Louise already has these skills in another form – training horses and riders to respond to one another. So although she naturally wants to move on from her hospital experience, while she still has to attend physiotherapy sessions she has the opportunity to bring out her strong social and interpersonal skills in an environment where she does not perceive her disabilities as marking her out from everyone else.

Once Louise completes her physiotherapy sessions the next step to improving her self-image could be to use her excellent communication skills in situations where her disability is not an issue for her. Using the phone is the obvious answer and there are many openings now available in paid employment which revolve around good telephone communication skills rather than meeting people face-to-face.

Her love of riding remains firmly entrenched. Providing similar pleasure to others with disabilities through extending and adapting facilities at her parents' riding stables is another option. There are charities who actively encourage disabled people to enjoy the experience of riding, and there is an obvious opening here for Louise to become directly involved.

During the time she has restricted mobility, Louise could invest in expanding her interest in antiques and ceramics by taking a course of study. This would develop the foundation skills she already has and could lead to other openings in the future.

How Louise can progress

In the longer term, Louise may be able to overcome her self consciousness sufficiently to be able to project her abilities   rather than her disabilities. By building on her secondary skills while regaining her confidence, she would not only extend her skills base, but would also improve her self-image at the same time.

Completing your portable skills audit

Just as you did with your social skills audit, use Worksheets 9, 10, 13, 16 and 24 to work from. Extract from these your portable skills, i.e. those that appear in more than one Worksheet, and list these on a separate page headed 'Portable skills'. Take each skill in turn and complete a separate Worksheet 26 for each of them. Again, if you find you have one or several portable skills which are being used more often than others, highlight these by making a separate list to draw attention to them.

Worksheet 26: Portable skills audit

Category of skill:

Instances of use and dates:

My strengths are:

My weaknesses are:

Areas I would like to improve:

I could improve these skills by:

Our next task in Chapter 8 will be to look at these skills with particular emphasis on how they can be put to use in the workplace and to study examples of how skills appear in many of the 'Job Vacancies' columns in the newspapers.

Summary

This chapter considered the use and value of transferable or portable skills to help you through a difficult patch in your life.

- You compared the skills you had recorded in your educational, home-based, pastime and occupational skills audits.
- You noted which skills you could identify as being used in more than one set of circumstances.
- To help understand why portable skills are the main planks of your life raft, you were also introduced to two case studies illustrating how portable skills can be used or adapted to meet changes in personal circumstances which demand seriously rethinking your lifestyle.
- You were asked to look at your portable skills separately and identify your strengths and weaknesses with a view to improving or developing them.

CHAPTER 8

Matching Skills to the Workplace

If you want to put your existing skills into a workplace environment, this chapter is devoted to that aim.

Many of the observations in the last chapter about lack of self-confidence apply equally in this chapter, particularly where in the past you may not have considered your existing skills to be relevant to the workplace. All too often, job applicants damn themselves by underplaying their hand in the way they complete their application forms, compile their CVs or – if they are lucky enough to get that far – present themselves at interview. Over-confidence is just as big a sin, of course, but an honest appraisal of what you might be capable of given the right circumstances should be your aim.

Changing times – changing roles

Today's employment market continues to adapt to meet the need to cut costs, improve competitiveness and thrive in an increasingly competitive marketplace. The profile of the workforce has changed too as a result of this tremendous upheaval and so have the expectations of what having a job really means. The most noticeable change has been a reduction in the number of jobs which will be 'for life' – or to be more precise, for your working life.

Over the last two decades or so, employers have had an expensive time delayering, downsizing and restructuring their organisations or businesses. Early retirements and redundancy payouts have not come cheap and the introduction of increasingly stringent employment legislation has meant it is now much harder to remove 'unwanted' employees without considerable cost.

To overcome legal constraints, new terms and conditions of employment have been devised to ensure an organisation can adapt quickly to changing circumstances, either by hiring people on a short-term casual basis, or by extensive use of short-term renewable contracts, part-time or temporary employment. This restructuring has resulted in more jobs on the market which suit women who are wrestling with the difficulties of having to work and run a home and family.

Women now make up around 50 per cent of the workforce, not only because of an increased desire to return to the workplace, but also through economic necessity as financial pressures to maintain living standards increase. At the same time there has been the second industrial revolution with the widespread use of technology in almost every workplace. The downturn in industrial activity and pressure on a range of middle management roles, both male-dominated areas, has forced men to rethink their working lives.

The loss of many traditionally male-orientated jobs has been counterbalanced by the huge rise in service industries, an area traditionally associated with female employment. Up until recently, men have not been attracted to part-time employment simply because it was perceived as the sort of work offered to, and only acceptable to, women. (Pretending such perceptions don't exist in an age of so-called equal opportunities unfortunately flies in the face of reality.) However, because there has been such a huge growth in this area of the jobs market and a reduction in the number of full-time jobs, there are signs of an increasing number of men who are now applying for part-time employment.

Another shift in emphasis, which has been touched on earlier, is the rise in the number of early retirements so that those who are still in employment up to the official retirement age are diminishing. In jobs where older and more experienced employees cost more, such as teaching for example, there has been a concerted effort to weed out those who are attracting higher salaries as part of a cost-cutting exercise. Many people over 50, and in some cases even over 40, have found themselves unemployed with little prospect of re-employment unless they are prepared to take lower-status lower-paid jobs. There are some employers who recognise the value of experience that comes with age who actively promote a policy of attracting older employees, but these are still a minority of businesses and they do not pay particularly high wages in any case.

Reading between the lines

> The basic skills people bring to the workplace are an increasingly varied mixture – from work, from home, from spare-time activities and from voluntary work.

These portable skills, which we discussed in the last chapter, are the key to opening doors into employment – and, for those who do not have any qualifications, offer the possibility of obtaining recognised National Vocational Qualifications which are skills and competency based.

As a way of helping you to think how your portable skills might be used to boost your job applications, we will once again be looking at some case studies. These will be used in conjunction with a selection of job advertisements taken from local papers. (The names of the businesses and their locations have been changed for the purposes of this book.) The adverts are set out on pages 140–41 and you may find it useful to keep a book mark in these pages for easy reference.

Case Study: Harry ────────────────────

Harry Dobson is in his late forties, married with a 21-year-old married daughter and two grandsons aged 2 and 3 years. Harry's wife has always been the homemaker and household manager, and now childminds their grandsons while their daughter is out at work.

Harry was educated at Fraymouth Secondary Modern School, staying on to get his CSEs, which included technical drawing, metalwork and woodwork. His hobbies at that time were linked into his father's interests and it was from him he learnt to service boat engines and the techniques needed to go sea fishing.

From school Harry went into Fraymouth Docks as an apprentice fitter following in his father's footsteps and by the age of 30 had become a foreman. Four years later the docks were closed and Harry was unemployed for two years before finding new employment at Railsford Rollingstock Ltd. After five years he was again made redundant with coachbuilding cutbacks. By then he was in his early 40s and found he could no longer find full-time employment. Since then he has taken both temporary and casual jobs to get out of the house and from under his wife's feet all day. These have included driving delivery vans for local firms.

Three years ago, one of Harry's friends persuaded him to help out the local

Sea Scouts who wanted someone experienced enough to instruct the cadets in designing and constructing a mock-up ship for the annual parade day. Harry discovered he had a good rapport with the youngsters and has been involved with them every since.

Harry has managed to save some of his redundancy money and has no serious financial problems, but he misses having a regular income he can rely on. He is toying with the idea of setting up a small engineering business of his own, servicing the tourist boats operating out of the old Fraymouth fishing harbour, but is not convinced this is financially viable. When he is not involved in some activity involving the Sea Scouts, as a casual hobby he creates ornamental metalwork pieces for friends and acquaintances, sharing a craft unit with an ex-workmate who is now self-employed as a wood-turner.

Harry's portable skills

Harry has a good range of portable skills:

- basic skills–literacy and numeracy;
- physical skills – all his faculties and good hand-to-eye coordination; driving ability;
- team skills – previous work situations required this;
- individual skills – metal and wood working, boat engine servicing, sea fishing;
- creative skills – modelling; designing and producing ornamental metalwork;
- supervisory and instruction skills – as foreman and as an instructor with the Sea Scouts;
- social skills – excellent social skills with peer group and young people;
- able to work on his own – driving the delivery vans.

Harry is right to have second thoughts about setting up his own business because he has no business or financial skills himself: the household management is his wife's responsibility; he was not involved in financial matters at work; he has no structured pricing policy for his metalwork and his contribution to the rental of the craft unit is on an informal basis.

Options for Harry

Although Harry has no business experience himself, his ex-workmate Bob is already self-employed and it might be beneficial

Expanding Local Company
has opening for

YOUNG PERSON
with practical ability

Excellent opportunity for someone
willing to start at ground level,
who shows enthusiasm and is able
to work as part of a team.

Write for application form to
RAILSFORD GARDEN CENTRE
Little Otterton
Railsford RF3 2GH

We have a fast-growing chain of 40 shops
selling quality gifts based on historical
themes and a thriving mail order business.
We also have a vacancy in our Railsford

 shop for a full-time

SALES ASSISTANT

With previous retail experience you
will relish the challenge of joining our
team and have strong merchandising
skills and the ability to deputise for
the manager in her absence.

To apply, please send your CV to:
Amy Yeo, Office Manager,
Presents from the Past,
22 Lower Square, Railsford RF1 6JQ

FRAY VALLEY DISTRICT COUNCIL
Leisure Services Department
Full-time Information Centre Assistants
required at the following centres
Town Hall, Railsford
Main Street, Winchampton
Market Street, Fraymouth

The work is challenging and rewarding and focuses on providing services for both local
residents and visitors. Essential qualities include an inquiring mind, good communication
skills and a sense of humour. Local knowledge of the Fray Valley area is essential and working
knowledge of at least one European language, preferably French, would be an advantage.

For further details and application form contact:

The Unit Manager, Leisure Services Unit
Fray Valley District Council, Town Hall, Railsford RF1 1AC
Tel: 0122 95959

DO YOU LIKE TALKING TO PEOPLE?
HAVE YOU A PLEASANT TELEPHONE MANNER?

If the answer to both is 'Yes', the Friends of Fray Valley Children's Hospice
are looking for part-time (8–10 hrs per week)

TELEPHONE CANVASSERS

to work from home to recruit volunteers for our Appeals Office
A home telephone is essential.
This is an interesting job which needs good
communication skills and accurate recording.
Full training will be given. Good rates of pay plus expenses.

For further details telephone Julie Latham on
0122 463798

Fig. 1. Examples of newspaper advertisements for job vacancies.

EDWARD FARRER & SON
Gorst Lane
Winchampton
RF18 9XR

We are looking for a
Full Time
MAINTENANCE ENGINEER
Must be skilled in working on
generators, small engines,
general garden machinery

To apply for interview phone
George Dean
012245 37156

MARTIN & HAWKBY
Solicitors, 6 Fish Street,
Fraymouth, RF15 6OP

TYPIST/CASHIER
wanted for a busy legal office and
building society agency.

It is essential you have audio-typing and
word-processing skills and an
understanding of general office duties. An
enjoyable post for someone with an
enthusiastic, out-going and friendly
personality. Applicants should write with
details of previous experience to

Mrs M Crawford at the above address.

FRAYSIDE COLLEGE
Currently undergoing restructuring to meet growing demand

ASSISTANT MANAGER
Business Development
Salary Range £11,800–£15,000

Required to take proactive and lead role in the development of business
opportunities for the College mainly in the areas of conferencing and letting of
facilities. Previous experience of commercial sector essential and HND/C in
Business Studies and Finance or equivalent desirable. Commitment and ability to
work as part of a team essential.

For further details and application form write to:

Harriet Barker, Personnel Officer, Frayside College,
Winchampton Road, Railsford RF2 5FQ

FRAYMOOR NATIONAL PARK

CLERICAL ASSISTANT
(Grade 1–5)

We need someone to provide typing and clerical services to our Park Management Staff. If you enjoy clerical
work and maintaining manual and computerised systems as well as some secretarial work, this job will appeal
to you. You will be proficient in office skills, including word processing and preferably hold RSA II
qualification. Good organisational and communication skills are essential, as is a flair for dealing with a varied
workload to stringent deadlines.

If you are an applicant with disabilities who meets the minimum requirements, we guarantee you
an interview.

For further details and application form send a large stamped, self-addressed
envelope to:
The Personnel Department, Fraymoor National Park Office,
Frayton Manor, Frayton, Railsford RF23 9SJ.

Fig. 1.   Continued

to both to make the craft unit a formal joint venture. Bob would continue to handle the financial side of the business while Harry could contribute his metal and woodwork skills, combined with his creative flair. In this way, Harry would be closer to the organisational side of running a business and it would give him the opportunity to see what financial and marketing skills were needed and whether these were skills he could acquire.

Alternatively, Harry could choose to apply for the job vacancy for a maintenance fitter advertised by Edward Farrer & Son (E in Figure 1 on page 141) using his portable skills.

Person specification for Maintenance Fitter

Edward Farrer & Son are a medium-sized tool hire firm operating out of Winchampton. They are a family business with a good reputation built up over three generations. They pride themselves in the quality of their service, which includes home delivery if requested, and are known to demand high standards from their 18 employees.

Their advertisement gives Harry several clues about the sort of person they want to employ.

1   There is no mention of the category of business Farrer's operate, or of their home delivery service. Only someone living in the Winchampton or Railsford area would know this, so they are looking for someone who lives locally. Because they operate a home delivery service, it is also likely they would be pleased to have someone who had driving skills. Harry meets both these requirements.

2   They are also looking for *skilled* applicants, so a younger person is less likely to have the range or depth of skills they want. This is a rare case where maturity will count for more than youth.

3   Application for interview has to be made by phone, so good communication skills will be needed which Harry has in abundance from his occupational supervisory and voluntary work instruction experience.

As with all job vacancy adverts, knowing as much as possible about the firm or organisation you are intending to apply to is as important as the information which appears in the advertisement itself.

Case Study: Brian —————————————————————————————

Brian Beeston is 51 years old, married, and has two children who are both in higher education. Although he lives in Winchampton, he is not from the local area. He was educated at a grammar school in the Midlands and left with three A levels. During his time at school he was a member of the successful school rugby teams for six years and in his last year was one of a group of prefects selected to act as guardians and role models for lower school pupils.

Going against the trend of his peer group, Brian decided against going to University and chose to go straight into employment as a clerk in a high street bank. He remained with this bank throughout his career, obtaining his professional qualifications and progressively climbing the promotional ladder until he became Corporate Business Manager based in Fraymouth when he was 48, a peripatetic role with a support staff of 5 based in a regional office. Two years later he was the victim of a massive restructuring and downsizing exercise. He was offered early retirement with a generous severance package which he gratefully accepted as he was finding that the intense pressure to meet targets was becoming more demanding than the job itself.

Having initially enjoyed the freedom from the work routine, he is now feeling slightly aimless and frustrated and would like to find some work to help ease the burden of his children's financial needs, particularly over the next two or three years. He is not worried about the prospect of loss of status, but thinks he might like to try his hand at something different.

Brian's spare-time interests have been dominated by those generated by meeting business clients in a social setting, such as golf and sailing, and from his involvement with his professional institute through local committee meetings and acting as Events Secretary for several years. Because his work was his life, he has lost touch with most of his friends outside the working environment and, since his retirement, has also lost touch with his business connections and colleagues. He knows he needs to start broadening his horizons in the immediate future to prepare for the time when he reaches the official retirement age and paid employment is not an option. ——————

Brian's portable skills

Brian's range of portable skills are all at a high level of competency:

- basic skills – literacy and numeracy;
- physical skills – all his faculties and good hand-to-eye coordination through golf and sailing;
- leadership skills – demonstrated at school and at work;

- management skills – a whole raft of skills here built up by years of experience in the bank:
  - communication both written and verbal
  - instructing and directing
  - administration
  - supervising and monitoring
  - encouraging and supporting (reinforced from school experience);
- organising skills – both at work and as Events Secretary for his professional institute;
- financial skills – excellent financial skills across a broad range of business categories and individual account needs;
- social skills – excellent interpersonal skills with professional peer group, corporate account customers and, from earlier experience, small to medium-sized business account customers and individual account holders;
- teamworking and individual abilities – both a good team player and capable of working on his own.

Brian's strengths are very much in his work skills, so if he intends to look for work he should be thinking seriously of putting these skills to use in a different environment.

Options for Brian

Brian needs work to meet his immediate concerns, i.e. to bolster his finances for the next two or three years until his children have both finished their higher education, and to widen his social circle.

With his range of financial skills, he could start up in business on his own as a financial consultant, but he has never had a burning desire to be self-employed. For this reason, he is probably right not to consider self-employment as an option.

As he has no set idea about what he would like to do, the best plan of action for him is to scour the local press to find job vacancies which would make use of his financial skills, preferably with some management element, but more importantly perhaps the opportunity to mix and meet with people again in a less intense marketing atmosphere. The advertisement placed by Frayside College for an Assistant Manager for Business Development (G in Figure 1 on page 141) could fit the bill.

Person specification for Assistant Manager

Frayside College used to be the local technical college and has been transformed into a college of adult and further education in the last eight years. Recently, under their new principal, the college has undergone further changes designed to make the best use of the buildings and facilities to earn extra income.

Their advertisement gives applicants a clear set of requirements to meet:

1 They are particularly looking for someone with marketing skills to initiate and develop business opportunities in conferencing and letting. Although Brian has not operated a business himself, he has seen the other side of the coin through his role as Corporate Business Manager and knows what is required to make a business successful. Initiating business was also a major part of his job, where he was expected to 'sell' the bank's financial packages to corporate customers.

2 The advertisement specifically asks for someone with experience in the commercial sector. Strictly speaking, Brian belongs to the financial sector, but his last job is sufficiently relevant to overcome any objection to him on this point.

3 Specific qualifications are quoted as being 'desirable'. Brian can more than match what is required.

4 Brian can demonstrate his commitment by virtue of his unbroken career in banking. His teamworking abilities can be illustrated not only through the skills required for his previous job, but also his membership of successive school rugby teams for six years.

Brian's most likely problem in applying to Frayside College will be the marked drop in salary he can expect to receive – which may well be a talking point during an interview. He will need to use his communication skills to some effect to satisfy his recruiters that it is the job which interests him and not the salary it commands.

Case Study: Simone

Simone Campbell is 30 and a single parent. She comes from a deprived area in Railsford and was taken into care when she was 12 as being beyond the care and control of her mother, who was also a single parent with two other children. Simone's education was minimal and despite the best endeavours of the local social services department and several foster parents, she continued to present behavioural problems. By the age of 15 she was already pregnant with her first child and had three more children by the time she was 21, all by different fathers.

Transferred to a new high-rise housing development in Railsford as part of an urban regeneration programme three years later, her life was dramatically changed by the death of Kitty, her youngest child, who was killed by a delivery vehicle while playing in the estate road outside the flats. She found support and help in the local church and became a convert, catching up on her literacy and communication skills through Bible reading classes and the mothers' meeting days.

Gaining in confidence, she organised a local crèche in the church hall with volunteer help and went on to lead a successful campaign for safe playing areas on the estate by making regular appearances on local television and radio. Using the experience she gained from this, she set up a Church-run organisation which provided holidays in the countryside for deprived youngsters and persuaded local employers to sponsor them. Once this was up and running on an annual basis, she widened her interests to include tenants' rights, representing the community at regular meetings with local councillors and officials of the housing department.

Simone has made sure her children have taken their education seriously and has taken casual part-time cleaning jobs so that she can be with them when they come home from school. Now they are all secondary school age, she is keen to find a permanent job to give herself more financial security but knows she may have difficulties gaining employment without previous work experience. Looking to the time when her children can look after themselves, she is beginning to think about taking a nursing or childcare qualification so that she can find full-time employment working with children. _____

Simone's portable skills

Simone's educational skills came long after her schooldays and the fact that she has managed to raise her educational standards herself is not just a credit to her motivation, but to her ability to learn. Her portable skills include:

- basic skills – self-taught literacy and numeracy;
- home-based skills – starting from a low skills base, she has developed and improved these to a high standard on all fronts as a single parent:
  - home maintenance

- household management
- caring and supporting skills in mother and child care;
- ◆ learning skills – a high level of ability to assimilate facts and figures as well as basic skills;
- ◆ organisational skills – extremely high level of competence here, evident in the success of her voluntary community work;
- ◆ communication skills – verbal skills amply demonstrated by her interviews on radio and television and her participation in the local housing forum meetings.

Options for Simone

Simone has already acquired a range of valuable skills through her home and community work which gives her a choice of possible careers. If she wanted to, she could start by taking a National Vocational Qualification (NVQ) in Childcare, as students can use their experience and demonstrable skills in unpaid work scenarios to complete the necessary competency units. This would give her a portable qualification which would enable her to take full-time employment as a nursery nurse.

However, Simone's abilities are very heavily weighted towards the organisational skills, so she has an alternative course of action she could follow. She may feel she could advance further by taking on organisational and administrative roles, although many employers may not accept her because of her lack of basic formal qualifications.

One way of overcoming this difficulty is by opting for a job which does not require formal qualifications, but skills. The vacancies for telephone canvassers (D in Figure 1 on page 140) for the Friends of Fray Valley Children's Hospice may provide such an opportunity. Networking is a powerful recruitment tool, and it is often possible to develop contacts as a result of one job which open the door to another once you have proved yourself capable.

Person specification for Telephone Canvasser

The Fray Valley Children's Hospice has just recently been opened and the Friends' group has been campaigning for many years to achieve this aim. They have a ten-bed facility with ancillary accommodation but would like to raise more money to build an additional wing for parents who have to travel long distances to visit their children and who need accommodation close to the hospice. The appeal for funding has just been launched and is being spread beyond the Fray Valley area to the surrounding districts which are eligible to send children to the hospice.

The Friends' advertisement concentrates on skills, not formal qualifications:

1   They pitch straight in with their headings: they want someone who likes talking to people and has a pleasant telephone manner. Simone has both these skills, amply demonstrated by her successes in her community work. The method of applying for the job will give her the chance to show off these skills to the full: the Friends have chosen the obvious method of recruitment in this case which is by telephoning Julia Latham for further details.

2   Persuasive skills are also being sought: the telephone canvasser is expected to be able to persuade others to join the group of volunteers running the Appeals Office. Simone has her ability to persuade other people demonstrated by her skill in getting employers to sponsor the countryside holidays for disadvantaged children and in getting her opinions accepted in the housing forums.

3   Accurate recording skills are also being asked for. Simone can substantiate her claim that she has these by producing the sponsorship file for the countryside holidays, together with the notes she has taken from tenants' meetings to the housing forums.

Not mentioned in the advertisement, but undoubtedly a plus in Simone's case, is her obvious interest in the welfare of children, which will make her approaches to other people sound genuine and sincere, and not just a 'sales pitch'.

Although this job is only part-time and will not be permanent, it does allow Simone the opportunity to build up her paid employment credentials. It could also lead through the training sessions to Simone being recognised as someone who would be suitable to recruit into one of the paid organisational administrative posts in the Friends' office should one become available.

Case Study: Kevin

Kevin Rhodes is 20. The youngest of three brothers, he has a family background dominated by parental conflict and negative attitudes to education and work. He is still living at home but both his older brothers have joined the Army.

Up until Kevin was 13, his grandfather provided parental guidance and Kevin spent a lot of time with him, particularly helping out on his allotment. He also encouraged Kevin to join his school under-14 football team which he enjoyed and provided him with an outlet from his disruptive home life. This steadying influence was lost when his grandfather died and without parental support Kevin quickly went off the rails. He dropped his interest in soccer and became part of a group of youngsters who regularly truanted from school and spent their time hanging around the goods yard in Railsford vandalising rolling stock and buildings, and in petty thieving from shops and cars.

When he officially left school at 16, he had no formal qualifications and only the basic literacy and numeracy skills he had been taught at junior school. Taking casual summer jobs as well as claiming unemployment benefit, Kevin shared a caravan with another mechanic and learned how to service engines with the Boats Round the Bay motor boat hire business operating from the fishing harbour at Fraymouth. He also earned extra cash at the pleasure beach as a stand-in funfair ride operator maintaining the generators.

A year ago, as part of a government training initiative for the long-term unemployed, he was allocated a place as a trainee groundsman with Fray Valley District Council working as part of a team in the Parks Department. Despite initial difficulties, he gradually settled to the work, enjoying being part of the team and using some of the skills he had gained from working with his grandfather. On the basis of this training he was taken on permanently, only to be made redundant a few months later as part of a cost-cutting exercise.

Disillusioned, Kevin went back to hanging around with a gang of other young men who stole cars on a regular basis. Although never involved directly in the thefts, he has removed engines and learned to drive although he has no licence or insurance. He has never been caught for these offences but has been arrested twice for drunken and disorderly behaviour. Two of the gang are currently serving prison sentences for car theft and drugs offences.

While out socially with his brothers who were on home leave, Kevin met up with a local girl. He has since repeatedly tried to set up a serious relationship with her but she has made it clear she finds his directionless lifestyle unacceptable. He now seriously wants to change and has no idea how to achieve this.

Kevin's portable skills

On the face of it, Kevin is one of life's losers who lacks the self-confidence and motivation to keep going when circumstances get tough. It is only now that he sees the only one who can change the situation is himself. Despite what appears on the surface to be little to build on, Kevin does have several good portable skills to help him:

- basic skills – literacy and numeracy at an unsophisticated level;
- physical abilities – good physical coordination skills from football, servicing and maintenance work;
- team skills – the more positive being his under-14s' role with the school football team and through his work with the Parks Department;
- learning skills – capable of learning through example;
- mechanical skills – maintaining engines and generators;
- horticultural skills – tending his grandfather's allotment and planting and maintaining public parks;
- social skills – limited, but he does respond positively in working environments.

Options for Kevin

Up until now, Kevin has had no goal in mind. His brothers have both suggested he join the armed forces to get him away from home and the no-hope environment he has allowed himself to be sucked into. This has no appeal for him even though he knows it would provide him with steady employment and the opportunity to get good training.

Kevin needs a job and he could apply for two of the advertisements (A and E in Figure 1 on pages 140–141) on the basis of the skills he already has. From his casual work and his period as a parks' groundsman he has all the skills being asked for to satisfy the requirements of a maintenance engineer for Edward Farrer & Son, although his experience with the generators and small engines was from casual undeclared work for which he could provide no proof or references. As a groundsman for Fray Valley District Council, however, he has both the references and experience needed to show he is capable of maintaining a range of garden machinery.

Kevin's other option is to try for the vacancy for the unspecified job with Railsford Garden Centre, although he may be older than the age range expected of would-be applicants.

Both jobs have other implications for Kevin. Farrers are based 20 miles away in Winchampton and travelling on a daily basis would prove too costly. This could provide Kevin with the ideal opportunity to break away entirely from the parental home and either take lodgings or find rented accommodation where he can start to shape his own life. Railsford Garden Centre is across town and would be easier for Kevin to reach. The pay is unlikely to be very good and he would have to continue to live at his parents' home at least for the foreseeable future.

Whichever job Kevin tries for, he needs to get two or three years of regular employment under his belt to consolidate the skills he already has, build on them and, if possible, add new ones so that he can open up opportunities for other employment alternatives in the future.

Person specification for Maintenance Fitter

This has already been discussed on page 142 and can be summarised as follows. The person they want to employ should

1 be skilled in maintaining generators, small engines and general garden machinery;
2 have good communication skills, presumably with customers; and
3 although not mentioned, should preferably have driving skills.

In Kevin's case, his real strengths are his mechanical abilities. If he is to apply for this job, he is going to have to brush up on his personal presentation skills which are very limited. His lack of a driving licence may be a stumbling block and Kevin will need to set his mind to putting this state of affairs on a proper footing.

If Kevin could persuade Farrers he has the potential to be a good employee, this job could provide him with steady employment using skills he already has to some degree.

Person specification for the vacancy with Railsford Garden Centre

Railsford Garden Centre has been developed over the last five years from a brown-field site. The present owners have stretched themselves financially to get the business going, but it has proved a success and they are now wanting to develop their business plan further. This involves regenerating a rough area behind the centre to use as a nursery, and extending the workshops to include a garden equipment servicing bay. They employ six staff who are multi-skilled, operating a rota system of running the retail outlet side, restocking and general maintenance of the building and grounds. Two of the six have specific horticultural skills. The expansion plans will stretch the existing staff on the maintenance and horticultural side and, until the financial returns from the new development come in, the owners can only afford to pay a relatively low wage to someone who can fill the gap.

The advertisement is non-specific in terms of what the job entails, but nonetheless it does provide pointers to the sort of person they want to employ.

1   The advertisement is looking for a 'young person'. This category almost certainly means a school leaver, probably 16–18 years of age looking for a starter job. This is reinforced by the pun 'willing to start at ground level'. There is no mention of any wage rate and the expected age of the applicant is likely to be reflected in what is offered. Kevin must expect only the minimum wage as a starting point.

2   Kevin's social skills and humour are not very sophisticated, so the clue about the 'cheerfulness' of any potential applicant suggested by the pun in the phrase 'willing to start at ground level' could well go unnoticed.

3   Regardless of whether or not an applicant should have a cheerful disposition, the two very specific skills required are 'enthusiasm' and 'ability to work as part of a team'. Kevin's ability to show enthusiasm is not very great, but he could certainly demonstrate his expertise in horticulture and maintenance. Also his casual work using mechanical skills could prove a plus point because of the centre's projected development plan. His ability to work as part of a team is easily proved by reference to his under-14 soccer team and his reference from the Parks Department.

Although on the face of it this job is not going to provide

Kevin with a long-term position, because the company is expanding there are likely to be other openings in the future. Kevin's skills are predominantly manual and technical, with a preference for the outdoor environment. If he can prove himself in the basic work at the centre and the business thrives, his longer-term prospects could include extending his skills base in horticulture and maintenance, with the possibility of becoming qualified through taking National Vocational Qualifications and later taking on supervisory roles as more staff are recruited.

Testing your skills identification abilities

So far in this chapter we have been looking at how individuals' life skills can help them find employment using some of the job vacancy advertisements on pages 140–41. Several of the advertisements have not been discussed yet.

Thinking about skills rather than qualifications, complete Tests 1–4 using these advertisements. Guidelines are at the end of the chapter on page 156.

TEST 1

B in Figure 1, page 140

SALES ASSISTANT – Presents from the Past

The skills needed for this job are:

TEST 2

C in Figure 1, page 140

INFORMATION CENTRE ASSISTANTS – Fray Valley Leisure Services

The skills needed for this job are:

Which skills would be essential?

Which skills would be useful but not essential?

TEST 3

F in Figure 1, page 141

TYPIST CASHIER – Martin & Hawkby

The skills needed for this job are:

Which skills are essential?

Which skills might be useful?

Which skills would you need to demonstrate your personality?

TEST 4

H in Figure 1, page 141

CLERICAL ASSISTANT – Fraymoor National Park

The skills needed for this job are:

Which skills meet the minimum requirements?

What additional skills might be useful?

Using your skills identification abilities

If you have some idea about the broad workstyle category of job you would like to do, such as those listed in Chapter 3:

- thinking
- organising
- administering
- doing

or the spheres of work you prefer, such as:

- dealing with people or animals
- manufacturing products
- managing finance
- working creatively

start collecting examples of job vacancy advertisements.

Using the format set out in Worksheet 27 which follows, and

the list of your portable skills identified on Worksheet 26, work out what skills are being asked for in job vacancy advertisements, match these with the skills you have, identify which skills need to be strengthened or adapted and what action you would need to take to be able to meet the requirements of the job.

Worksheet 27: Matching personal skills to job vacancies

Title of job:		
Skills needed:	Level required (basic, good or excellent:	Essential/additional or useful (state which):
Skills in my possession:	Level of skill (basic, good or excellent):	
Skills matched:		
Skills matched but not at the level required:		
How could I improve my level of competency in these skills?		
Skills not matched:		
How could I go about getting these skills?		

Improving your occupational skills base

With so much emphasis on the importance of skills in the workplace these days, there are numerous sources of help to improve your skills which can be tapped into, for example:

◆ Jobcentres
◆ Training and Enterprise Councils (TECs), Local Enterprise Companies (LECs) in Scotland
◆ careers service providers
◆ further or adult education colleges or departments of adult education at universities
◆ Department for Education and Employment (DfEE)

and these can all be found in your *Phone Book*. With the increasing use of the internet, if you have access to this, you will find many training providers as well as government departments operate websites. At any one time there are usually several government sponsored training initiatives available but these tend to change quite frequently as do the criteria for being eligible to qualify for them.

> If you have the motivation to achieve more, the means of achieving it are readily available.

Guidelines to skills tests answers

Test 1

Sales assistant skills needed are: numeracy, strong merchandising skills, teamworking ability, communication skills, social skills, potential managerial skills.

Test 2

Information centre assistant skills needed are: *essential* – literacy, research skills, good verbal communication skills, social skills, teamworking abilities; *useful,* – linguistic skills in French or other European language.

Test 3

Typist cashier skills needed are: *essential* – manual dexterity, literacy, audio-typing and word processing, numeracy, financial handling and recording, basic administration; *useful* – teamworking ability, being able to understand legal terminology, being able to follow verbal and written instructions correctly – tea and coffee making; *to demonstrate your personality* – social skills, good communication skills with particular reference to your excellent tea and coffee making abilities – a sense of humour is an asset when it is played with a light touch.

Test 4

Clerical assistant skills needed are: *minimum requirements* – manual dexterity, word processing to RSA II level, organisational skills, good communication skills, time management skills; *additional* – shorthand or note-taking skills, IT skills in general.

Summary

Chapter 8 looked at the changing face of the world of work over the recent past and the effect on the jobs market.

- You were shown how skills are playing a greater part in job vacancy advertisements.
- You were introduced to four case studies to help you understand the options available for employment in each case by reference to examples of job vacancy advertisements.
- The remaining examples of advertisements were considered and you were asked to identify the skills being sought.
- You were also encouraged to start matching your own skills to a self-selected set of job advertisements which were relevant to the particular sphere of work you might be interested in.
- You were expected to identify any shortcomings in your skills base and what you intended to do to overcome these.

*It's good to be out
on the road, and
going one knows
not where.*
MASEFIELD:
THE TEWKESBURY
ROAD

CHAPTER 9

Continuing Personal Development Outside Employment

T he concepts of lifelong learning which became the vogue of the 1990s are now firmly established. Employees are encouraged to take on board their own development; employers expect a multi-skilled and flexible workforce. The emphasis lies heavily on how people who are out of work can be brought back into the workplace, and government initiatives continue to be concentrated in this area. There is nothing wrong with these concepts: our society as a whole depends on having as many people as possible economically active to support those who are not.

There is a problem, however, with the terminology of 'lifelong learning'. In most cases when this concept is being discussed it becomes clear that what is being referred to is not *lifelong* learning but *worklong* learning – the 30–40 years when you might be economically active. What keeps slipping out of sight in the glow of enthusiastic rhetoric is the question – where does this leave those who are leaving the workforce early, for whatever reason good or bad, and who may or may not be able to return to it at a later stage? If you belong to this category, this chapter is particularly for you. We will be looking at the situation which faces those above the official retirement age in Chapter 10.

Getting the best out of life

Going out to work provides us with a structured framework for living, not quite so rigidly nine-to-five as it might have been in the past, but structured nonetheless. Once this structure is taken away, reaction to its loss depends on the individual's perception of what has caused the loss and whether they had any role to play in the process that led up to it. Someone who has been made redundant is likely to have a very different perspective on what has happened from someone who has decided on a career break or taken voluntary early retirement. For this reason, there may be a wide range of diverse emotions: a sense of anger or relief, bitterness or jubilation.

What is important for anyone coming out of the workplace before reaching the official retirement age is the possibility, however remote in some cases, that they will at some stage get back into work at a future date. For this reason alone it is important to keep what skills you have, and more importantly perhaps, to build on these, or start adding new ones to your collection.

There are other reasons, of course, which are just as important. These are:

- nurturing your self-esteem
- maintaining your self-confidence
- fostering your health and well-being.

Nurturing your self-esteem

> There is so much emphasis on the importance of having a job that it is difficult not to feel disadvantaged among your peer group if you do not have one.

It is also extremely difficult not to find yourself in the uncomfortable position of feeling it is necessary to explain away the situation – of being almost apologetic for your lack of employment.

This sense of being an 'unperson' can be very strong and it is not helped by the constraints of having less money to spend and of not being able to take part in as many social activities as you did previously. There are after all very few social activities which do not involve spending money. In this situation, you not only lose the status which a job automatically confers on you, but you also have the potential for losing contact with your friends as well. With all these negative inputs, how can you nurture your self-esteem?

The most obvious answer in the first instance for someone who has been actively building their skills life raft, is to spend some time rereading their Personal Resource Pack. One of the main reasons for exploring your life skills, remember, is to provide you with a safety net when life takes a turn you don't expect. Of course, it is not always easy to think positively or feel a glow of achievement over previous triumphs, particularly if you are feeling depressed or anxious: there can even be the tendency to sink ever further into the slough of despond precisely because everything you have ever achieved in the past has led you to this point in your life. This is not so of course, because your skills and achievements are a part of you, and your portable skills particularly are the shining beacons to light your way forward.

Maintaining your self-confidence

A sense of insecurity often leads to a conscious or unconscious decision to pull back from meeting other people. Once this becomes a habit, it can reinforce itself until you become isolated in your own world with nothing to stimulate you or take your mind off your problems. This in turn reduces your interpersonal skills which increases your loss of confidence and you are caught up in a vicious circle with no obvious way out.

Nurturing your self-esteem is the first step in maintaining your self-confidence. If you value who you are and what you have to offer, you cannot help but feel this inner sense of self-worth working to your advantage.

One of the most positive ways to keep your self-confidence in good trim is by exercising your social skills. This does not necessarily involve 'socialising' and can be achieved simply by talking to other people on a day-to-day basis: the milkman, postman, shopkeeper, check-out girl, the old man walking his dog in the park – all those people who probably do not know anything about you or the problems you are facing. What is crucially important in these circumstances is to talk about anything which has nothing to do with what is worrying you, because in this way you keep your mind open to a broader range of concerns than those which are trying to dominate your thoughts.

Fostering your health and well-being

You cannot feel positive about life if your physical health is not good and your state of mind is permanently locked into a negative operating mode.

You don't have to pay expensive gym fees to stay healthy and not everyone has a vegetable patch to dig over or a lawn to mow. Jogging is an option, but the simplest and most envigorating activity is a brisk walk: it tones up the system; increases blood flow to the brain and costs absolutely nothing. If you can vary your route and try to bring some diversity into the ritual, so much the better.

Your diet is just as important. Plenty of variety with as much unprocessed food as is practical is the ideal to aim for, but so is monitoring how much you eat. Eating too much is as harmful as eating too little. Too much food or drink reduces the ability to get up and go generally, and encourages not just a stodginess in appearance but of thought processes as well. Equally, becoming obsessive about putting on weight for fear of becoming a couch potato is just adding more anxieties into your life which you can do without. It is better to allow yourself the occasional luxury of comfort food to bolster flagging spirits, or as a reward for rereading your PRP and reminding yourself just how much you have to offer.

Leading an active life goes a long way to keeping our mental state in good order. But you can't be on the go all the time and it is on those occasions when you are relaxing on your own that black thoughts have a nasty habit of intruding. Brooding on situations is a solitary activity and you can't always summon up an understanding soul-mate at the drop of a hat. The answer is to identify your personal counterbalance to negative thoughts: it may be the TV, radio, listening to music, playing an instrument, reading or doing crosswords. But whatever your personal pacifier is, use it. Very often you will find that your subconscious will work through the problem for you and you will be better able to cope the next time around.

Keeping your mind active

In the world of today's professional, there is a process known as *continuing professional development* (CPD): it is part of the concept of 'worklong' learning.

Once upon a time you could qualify in this or that, obtain a certificate or diploma, put it on the wall and go off and do whatever it was you were qualified to do. In a relatively static working environment where change was slow and incremental, this was no great problem, but as the speed of change quickened in every sphere of work towards the end of the 20th century, it became increasingly necessary to update working practices on a regular basis.

CPD or its equivalent is becoming increasingly commonplace, and the requirement is laid on professionals to continuously seek ways of improving and developing their professional performance; to prove that they are doing this, and if they are not, to be encouraged to do so. The ultimate sanction for not doing so is the loss or removal of that professional status.

For someone outside the world of work the imperative to do something similar is just as strong – in this case to engage in continuous *personal* development. In this way the skills which have been acquired are nourished, used and kept up to date, or built on to a new level of competency; or new skills are tried and developed to broaden the range of skills available to you when you want to return to work.

> Your brain should be given stimulus to continue functioning to the best of its ability.

Your little grey cells may be dying off, but it is now accepted that the more you use them, the slower the rate of deterioration in your mental faculties. In a nutshell – use them or lose them.

Choosing new directions to follow

At the start of this chapter we highlighted the emphasis on initiatives devised to bring latent skills back into the workplace. This chapter looks at the other side of the same coin – of bringing work skills back into the home or community to the benefit of yourself and everyone who needs these skills.

Open any local newspaper and you will see column inches by the mile devoted to the activities of local groups, charities or organisations covering just about any topic you care to mention. Beside them are the regional branches of national or international charities with their defined aims and objectives well known to everyone. If you add into these the diverse range of voluntary work associated with, for instance, education, health, social services, the police and the prison service; unpaid public service such as school governors and independent persons on tribunals; service on local councils or as members of parliament, it becomes increasingly clear that all these activities require skills and expertise of every sort.

You may, of course, already spend time on voluntary work, but if your pastimes are more to do with your own interests, now's the time to branch out and add in a different dimension to what you are doing.

As usual, your portable skills will provide you with the obvious pointers. No organisation is likely to turn away anyone who has a skill to offer which they can make use of. For example, there is almost always a shortage of administrative and financial skills in any groups which have a formal structure. Anyone who is willing to sit on a committee, take notes, write letters, become treasurer or be available to give a talk on the work of the group is likely to be welcomed with open arms. Fund-raising and marketing skills are eagerly sought by groups wanting to improve and develop the services they offer. Practical skills such as driving, painting and decorating, gardening and shopping, are a gift to those organisations dedicated to helping the elderly or infirm. Interpersonal and communication skills are vital to groups offering advice and guidance to others. Organisational skills are valued by just about everybody.

When choosing where to offer help, think about the sort of organisation you would feel comfortable with. Look at your pastimes audit (Worksheet 24) and see the types of activity you have gone for in the past. Are these:

◆ formal or informal;
◆ group or one-to-one;
◆ devoted to a particular cause or several;
◆ working with adults, children or animals;
◆ involving indoor or outdoor activities;
◆ aimed at the able-bodied or disabled; or
◆ the sick or terminally ill?

If you have never felt at ease in a structured organisation, there are still options open to you on an informal basis: providing company for someone who is housebound; helping a friend decorate their home; looking after your neighbour's goldfish while they are away; making tape recordings of articles in the local paper for the blind; writing letters for someone badly handicapped by arthritis – the list is practically limitless. All you need is the motivation to give your skills to help someone else.

Whatever you choose, you will discover very quickly that there are several benefits which accrue automatically:

1 Becoming involved stops you thinking too much about yourself.
2 Other people's difficulties often put your own into a better perspective.
3 Meeting different people keeps your social skills alive and well.
4 Putting your skills to use keeps them in shape.

Giving your time to voluntary work can also give you the chance to try your hand at a new skill without the pressures you would be under if you were in paid employment. This applies too if you decide to take on a greater level of responsibility. If you succeed, you have the comfortable knowledge that you have developed your skills base. If you find you have bitten off more than you can chew, it is not going to blight your career if you say so.

Depending how your circumstances turn out, you may find your career break or 'time out' improves the quality of your life in unexpected ways, or provides you with a new direction you might never have thought of before. More importantly for those who do not return to work, it provides a more satisfying and stimulating lifestyle which can be carried on into official retirement and the remaining 30 or 40 years of their lives.

Case study: Caroline

Caroline James is 35. She did well academically at school in all her arts subjects and was extremely popular because of her extrovert personality. She enjoyed taking part in the school drama productions both on stage and as one of the set designers. In her final year she was Head Girl and one a team of three who represented the school in a national debating competition. After leaving school she went on to study law and politics at university where she also joined a political student group. After receiving her honours degree she went on to qualify as a solicitor and joined a practice in Railsford which specialised in defending criminal cases. There she built up an impressive reputation and three years later, aged 26, she married Geoffrey, another solicitor in the same practice and they currently live in a small hamlet on the outskirts of Winchampton which does not have the benefit of public transport.

Caroline and her husband took the decision to defer having a family until her career was firmly established. The original plan was for her to take maternity leave and then return to the practice full-time once they had the services of a nanny. Three months ago when Simon was born Caroline changed her mind about returning to work immediately. Both she and her husband are now considering having another child once Simon is a year old, and possibly other children in the longer term. Caroline is now of the opinion that she would not want to return to work before all her children reached secondary school age.

Since she has been at home, Caroline has renewed her former hobby of pencil drawing which she can fit in between the demands of a small baby. At the moment her life revolves around him most of the time but she recognises that although she is happy in the role of mother, she still needs a high input of mental stimulus which childcare on its own does not give her. Her husband is very supportive of her decision to remain at home but recognises she will need to occupy herself in whatever spare time she has in a way which will provide the stimulus she needs.

Caroline's decision to take an extended career break means a rethink on how best she can use her skills base to provide the necessary stimulus, while allowing her to put her family to the forefront of her life while the children are still very young. _____

Caroline's portable skills

Caroline has a range of high-level skills at her disposal:

- basic skills – literacy is particularly good;
- physical skills – good hand/eye coordination, all her faculties and she can drive;
- individual skills – capable of working to a high level of competence on her own initiative;
- organisational skills – demonstrated by her skills in accruing evidence to present in court;
- analytical skills – borne out by her ability to structure cases in a coherent way for presentation in court;
- communication skills – excellent communication skills demonstrated both in court and by her previous contribution to the debating team and drama productions at school, and

her involvement with the political group at university;

♦ social skills – excellent interpersonal skills which have always been evident through her extrovert personality;

♦ creative skills – demonstrated by her drawing, painting and set designing;

♦ leadership skills – a good ability to act in leadership roles demonstrated while at school as Head Girl and in the debating team.

Options for Caroline

While her children are young, Caroline may have to accept that most of her uninterrupted spare time in the first years will be predominantly in the evenings when they are in bed. Once they are all at school, however, which could be eight or nine years ahead, she will have more time during the day, at least during the school term.

Caroline's skills are a mixture of the solitary and the social. This range fits in well with her new lifestyle. She also has the benefit of being able to drive so she is not isolated and could choose to think in wider terms than the hamlet where they live.

The most obvious type of activity for Caroline should involve the use of her organisational, analytical, communication and interpersonal skills which are her great strengths. Initially, with her time at a premium, voluntary organisations such as the Citizens' Advice Bureau would be an obvious starting point. She also has the ability to speak in public and once Simon joins a playgroup she could consider going into local schools to give talks on the workings of the legal system or what is involved in being a defending solicitor in criminal cases.

Her next option picks up on her previous interest in politics. There is always a need for good quality candidates to represent local people at all levels of local government. She could either start by becoming involved at a parish level, or if this is too narrow for her interests, she could become an active member of her local political party with a view to being selected at some time in the future to stand as their candidate either in the district or county elections. This would provide her with an environment which would suit her while giving her the opportunity to expand her skills in a slightly different way from using them in the court room, while at the same time keeping her court room skills in trim ready for the time she may wish to return to work.

Being a councillor, however, demands not just regular attendance at full council meetings, but also taking part in committees and sub-committees. The amount of paper generated can be mountainous and, to be effective, a councillor has also to set aside time to digest the information provided in agendas and reports. If she felt her time was too limited to take on board the heavy commitment of being a councillor while the family was still very young, any formally structured society or group would welcome her organisational skills. It will be up to Caroline to decide which of the many voluntary organisations or charities she would like to associate with and what role or roles she could fulfil to their best advantage.

In the meantime, until she has made her decision about what she would like to do in the longer term, her previous interest in drama as well as her communication skills could provide her with an outlet for her creative talents with amateur dramatic or operatic groups, either on stage or in designing sets for their productions.

All of these activities would provide Caroline with the essential mental stimulus she needs to be fulfilled as a person in her own right. Her involvement would also ensure that she maintained her skills, with the possibility of finding new options to pursue through having a wider selection of networks to access than she has had previously.

Case study: Mark _____

Mark Palmer is 32. He left university with an honours degree in chemistry but without any real idea what sort of job he wanted. He became a salesman with a large pharmaceutical company when his attempts to find a pure research opening came to nothing and two years later married his long-term girlfriend.

Mark was never at ease as a salesman. Increasingly the pressures of the job and the long absences away from home were putting a strain on his marriage. After five years, his wife left him and moved back to live with her parents in Scotland, taking their two young sons with her. The divorce settlement involved selling the matrimonial home in Winchampton and there were insufficient funds left over for Mark to buy another property. He rented a small house in Railsford but spent little time there, trying instead to keep out on the road as much as possible to improve his sales figures. After six months he suffered a nervous breakdown, his mental recovery hampered by physical ill-health including hypertension and bouts of bronchitis exacerbated by his high level of smoking. After an extended leave of absence, his contract with his employers was terminated. He is still receiving regular medical and psychiatric monitoring for hypertension and depression.

Mark is essentially a thinker rather than a doer and should have been advised to keep looking for a research post rather than choosing a career which was so totally at odds with his motivation and personality. At school he had always been a steady worker who did better when faced with longer time scales and less pressure. He was not particularly sociable, always on the fringe of a larger group of classmates, and because he was not physically robust was never involved in any of the school sports teams. Out of school his hobbies had included making models, reading science journals and astronomy. This pattern continued during his time at university but once he started work he had neither the time nor the energy to pursue any spare-time activities at all.

Mark is likely to be out of the employment market for some time, a thought which in itself frightens him and makes his depression worse. He now rarely sees his sons and does not know where to turn to give meaning to the rest of his life. _____

Mark's portable skills

Mark's stronger skills are his academic ones, but this should not be allowed to overshadow his other abilities, even if these are lower in his own perception:

- basic skills – literacy and numeracy to a high level;
- specific skills – understanding chemistry to degree level and a higher than average knowledge of astronomy;
- physical skills – good coordination, dexterity in particular through his modelling;
- individual skill – capable of working on his own but at his own speed;
- analytical skills – through studying science subjects;
- social skills – somewhat limited and not helped currently by his depression;
- creative skills – model making, even though this is sometime in his past;
- marketing skills – moderately good, but these do not come naturally;

♦ communication skills – again, moderately good because of his sales training, but he can express himself well on topics which interest him.

Options for Mark

Mark's first priority will have to be to regain his physical and mental health – and the two are sometimes inextricably bound together – an improvement in one can often help to induce an improvement in the other. His self-confidence is understandably at an all-time low and, until his sense of self-esteem improves, this too will inhibit his recovery.

To some extent, Mark's devotion to work to the exclusion of all else has impoverished his skills base, and this has not been helped because the skills associated with his work are not his strongest. To build up his confidence he should consider using those skills where he succeeded in the past and use them in such a way that he can feel he is being of some use to someone else.

The most obvious of his talents is his ability to understand scientific subjects. With his qualifications and his ability to communicate well on topics which interest him, he could consider providing one-to-one tuition for young people wrestling with their GCSEs or A Levels. This is a very positive atmosphere to operate in and has none of the threatening overtones of competitiveness associated with the pressures of selling. He would also be in charge of the timescale which would reinforce his need to become more in control of his own life. There would be the additional benefit of improved self-worth which comes with helping other people to succeed.

On a longer-term basis, Mark could join a modelling club to widen his range of acquaintances and lift his social skills. In this way, he would help to improve his chances of discovering other interests through club members which in turn would lead to other openings. Modelling is also one of the many varied activities which young people can take as part of the Duke of Edinburgh Award Scheme. Once he has gained confidence in his role as a tutor, Mark could well offer himself as a volunteer instructor to youth organisations who run Awards' programmes. Again, this is an opportunity for improving self-esteem through helping others while at the same time acquiring a new skill – instructing. By building on older skills, Mark may eventually be fit enough to return to the workplace in a capacity which better suits his natural abilities and motivation.

Drawing up your own Continuing Personal Development Plan (CPDP)

If you are in the position of coming out of the workforce sooner than you expected and really don't know what to do, you need to indulge in a spot of focused brainstorming.

1   Read through Worksheets 17–23 on your spare-time interests – all of them – including those you have not followed for many years. Think about them. What are your main interests? Record these on your Continuing Personal Development Plan as set out on page 171 in Worksheet 28.

2   Are there any other interests you would like to have explored if time/money/energy/opportunity had permitted? Think about these and record them on your CPDP too.

3   Read through Worksheet 26 on your portable skills. Think about these in relation to your stated interests. Could you use these skills in any way in conjunction with your interests? How would you achieve this? Would you need any additional knowledge, skills or training? Note this down on your CPDP as well.

4   Set yourself a target date to complete your investigation of the possibilities you have identified and note this on a calendar.

5   Monitor your progress on the due date and set another date for the next review if this is necessary, noting this date on the calendar too.

6   Check your priorities have not changed in the interim and if they have, make whatever adjustments are necessary to your CPDP.

Worksheet 28: Continuing Personal Development Plan

My main interests are:

I would like to try:

I could use my portable skills with these interests in the following ways:

To do this I would need to:

How can I go about achieving this?

| Review dates |

Summary

Chapter 9 looked at ways to open up unexpected opportunities for you to follow outside the workplace using your existing skills.

- You were asked to think about alternatives by building on older skills which might be in abeyance.
- You were encouraged to get the best out of life by nurturing your self-esteem, maintaining your self-confidence, and fostering your health and well-being.
- The importance of keeping your mind active was brought to your attention.
- Ideas were put forward as to how you should choose new roads to follow with particular reference to voluntary work.
- You were introduced to two more case studies involving people coping with long-term changes in their lives and the possible options open to them.
- To help you decide what direction to take, you were encouraged to complete a Continuing Personal Development Plan.

CHAPTER 10

Looking Beyond Employment

M uch of the thrust of government thinking over the recent past has been to encourage people to look at their lives as a continuous learning process. We are now expected to involve ourselves in lifelong learning. But, as we touched on in the last chapter, too often the emphasis on this learning seems to get bogged down in restricting the activity to those who are economically active in the workplace.

It may be at some time in the future, when the generation which is in work now comes to the official retirement age, that they will be so imbued with the concept of continuing to learn throughout their working lives and the need to keep their skills constantly honed, the habit will continue beyond the world of work. But in the meantime around 11 million people in this country belong to what is now known as 'The Third Age'. This is the age beyond full-time employment and parental responsibility.

There is a delightful anarchic image of irresponsibility in this definition of Third Age which conjures up lines of poetry about growing old disgracefully, wearing purple and learning to spit. But there is an element of freedom from responsibility in later life which, for the more imaginative or the adventurous of spirit, does allow you the opportunity to escape from a lifestyle dominated by constraints of employment or parenthood – or both. It can be a time of pursuing new ideas, resurrecting old interests – of being daring in some way you might never have envisaged.

Giving new meaning to life

In the past it was not uncommon for men (and it was usually men in this instance) to retire from their work and to be dead within a year of their retirement. They simply stopped living. The work ethos was so deeply ingrained that it represented the full meaning of their lives – their reason for living. Once they lost their economic purpose, they had nothing else to fall back on: they did not recognise that although the job may have come to an end, the skills they took to that job for 40 years or more were still with them.

If there has been some benefit from the recessions and company reorganisations we have had in this country over the last two decades which have so radically altered the profile of the world of work, it must be that it has forced us all to rethink how to get the best out of life as a whole, and not just while we are likely to be economically active. And, as has been touched on several times already in this book, as we all tend to live longer, we need to have some idea how to tackle what could well be half our life-span beyond the world of work.

By the end of the 20th century, 50 per cent of men over the age of 50 were no longer part of the workforce for one reason or another, and it is estimated that by 2050 it will have become commonplace for three generations within the family to be retired: the newly retired 50-year-olds, their parents in their seventies and their grandparents – the ever increasing number of people living to become centenarians.

For some of the younger 'retired' group, the answer to the question of how to fill their lives has been to seek re-employment either on a full-time or part-time basis. Others have chosen self-employment, using previous skills as a basis for setting up as consultants. For others this course of action has been either impractical or, because they have no economic imperative to return to work, they have actively chosen to find fulfilment in other ways.

> For some people 'retirement' is a welcome relief from the stresses and strains of employment.

All they want to do is relax, socialise, spend some of their retirement money on exotic holidays, play golf or sit watching TV. There is nothing wrong with this, but ultimately the question has to be asked – can you do this for the next 40 or 50 years of your life? The answer is almost always 'No'. The possible reasons why this lifestyle will be impossible to maintain are:

◆ boredom
◆ lack of funds

- ◆ infirmity
- ◆ ill-health.

Slipping into boredom

Having a job injects a large slice of activity into our lives as well as a social structure. The majority of interaction between colleagues revolves around the processes of the job. Once the job is taken out of the picture, not only is the occupation lost, whole areas of daily conversation drop away at the same time.

Attempts to fill both gaps by simply doubling up the time you spend on your existing spare-time interests does not always work in the longer term. Initial enthusiasm for meeting friends or playing rounds of golf every day can pale over time if the contributions to the conversation become limited. Tales of 'the one that got away' after a day's fishing, the difficulties of putting on the 16th green, or enthusing about the grandchildren are all part of social interaction between people, but there is a limit to how often these can be discussed fruitfully on a regular basis.

The need to 'liven things up' makes gossips of us all in our attempts to put something new into our social gatherings. The more times we meet the same people, the more difficult it becomes to say something interesting. When we have exhausted our exchange of mutually interesting topics, we fall back on trivia and the quality of our social experience starts to reduce in value. We become bored.

If we can be bored ourselves, we can be just as guilty of boring other people: we dominate the conversation with details of family, holidays or other topics which are irrelevant to our listeners, either because they don't know the people involved, or have no equivalent experience to provide a counterbalance to our monologue. This capacity to bore others is not intentional: it is often the result of having nothing else to say of general interest. We have, if we are truthful, exhausted our reserves of useful conversation.

Boredom is perhaps more usually associated with someone who is on their own with no mental or social stimulus. Sitting watching TV for hours on end is often seen as an alternative to having the company of other people. Unfortunately, unlike listening to the radio where you can continue to do the cooking, your model making or whatever at the same time, you cannot do this type of activity while watching TV. If you watch a lot of TV during the course of a day, you are restricting yourself to long periods of inactivity.

> Inactivity over long periods is bad for your physical state of health.

As your body gets older it needs to be treated with consideration. This means keeping reasonably active to keep heart and lungs in good working order and to prevent joints from stiffening up prematurely. Inactivity also dulls mental faculties, as anyone who has tried to concentrate on a demanding mental task for a long period knows only too well. The thought processes become sluggish after about half an hour, and after an hour taking a break becomes essential if any further progress is to be made.

It is almost certain that after a while, you will no longer want to continue in the way you began at the start of your retirement. You will find boredom creeping in, and you will want to do something about it.

Facing up to financial limitations

Without doubt, if you have not made adequate provision for your Third Age the future will stop looking very rosy very quickly. Only the lucky few will be able to continue with the regular expensive or exotic holiday regime beyond 10 or 15 years.

Admittedly most of the heavy expenditure will be a thing of the past: the mortgage will have been repaid; the children will have completed their education and struck out on their own. But you only have to look at how the value of money has eroded over the past 30 years to see what the potential is for something similar to happen again during the later years of your life. You need to be confident that what you are doing with your life is not going to be a course of action which leads to an impoverished old age.

Discovering infirmity

Infirmity is not ill-health: it is the gradual process of ageing which reduces our capacity to do things we used to take for granted. You discover you can no longer run for the bus as quickly as you used to; your back aches more when you have been sitting for a long time; your eyes don't see as well as they did; your hearing is becoming woollier, and so on. It doesn't usually happen overnight: it creeps up on you bit by bit.

Those activities you choose to do when you begin retirement may not be sustainable over a longer period and to invest too heavily in these may blunt your ability to investigate sooner some alternative pastimes with a longer 'sell-by date'.

Accepting ill-health

Ill-health is not the preserve of the elderly, and not everyone who is old has ill-health as a matter of course. Many people nowadays do enjoy a very vigorous and vital old age. But the likelihood of developing an illness of some sort does come with advancing years.

Like infirmity, it may be little more than an inconvenience, or it can be debilitating. Unlike infirmity, which can often be overcome by using some sort of aid to help with walking, seeing, hearing etc, ill-health saps the strength and can often sap our willingness to reduce its impact by diversionary tactics. The art is to have in place a range of interests that will help to take your mind away from whatever you are coping with, even if this is only for short periods of time at a stretch.

The quality of your life is all important.

Considering the options

The trick to enjoying a more stimulating and rewarding Third Age, is to plan well ahead, not in any hard and fast way, but to have a rough idea what you would like to do over the next ten years, the ten years after that and so on.

In Chapter 9 you looked at the skills and interests which have made up your life so far. This is precisely the same approach to use now, only this time you are not looking at the possibility, however remote, that you will be returning to the workplace. This is the opportunity for you to rediscover and revitalise dormant skills and to branch out into new ones, however outrageous, and go for it. Don't let your existing skills atrophy through neglect only to find they let you down when you need them most once the first flush of retirement euphoria has died away.

As we discovered earlier, boredom can be experienced when you are on your own or with others. It is a very negative experience and keeping it at bay has to be a priority.

Taking your skills into the community

One of the most satisfying courses of action is to use your work skills productively within the community.

It is perhaps one of the saddest facts of life that enthusiasm or dedication alone is no longer enough to satisfy the requirements needed to serve on some of the organisations which exist within our society. Rightly or wrongly, a professional approach is now essential for some bodies to function to the level expected of them. This is largely because they are increasingly regulated by statute, or in some cases set up by statute with very specific duties and responsibilities. Take, for example, the setting up of independent review or appeals' panels to deal with complaints arising from the way social services departments or schools are operating, or the selection of lay members involved in employment tribunal hearings.

These quasi-judicial bodies need people who not only have the time but also the right sort of skills to evaluate evidence on which to make good quality decisions. Selection procedures in some cases now involve not only attending the expected interview, but also sitting a battery of psychometric tests to check that your personality and skills level matches the 'person specification' identified as essential for the requirements of the role.

As the numbers of monitoring bodies increase and their remits are more and more set down in either statute or regulation, the need for people who have the right sort of skills to bring to these bodies rises too. The greatest pool of expertise lies with those who have just come out of the workplace, and it is this group who will be increasingly sought after to provide the much needed combination of skills and available time to make these bodies function effectively.

In other situations, such as the composition of governing bodies for schools and colleges for example, it is no longer simply desirable to have a core of members who are well-versed in financial control and budgeting, it has become essential. But financial skills are not the only ones which are now needed as a matter of course. Governing bodies are now very much in the business of managing the school or college, responsible for every area with the exception of the management of day-to-day functions. So beside the more obvious management skills which are needed, other skills being sought include:

- personnel skills needed to operate recruitment, selection and disciplinary codes of practice;
- technical skills needed to understand health and safety provisions, access arrangements for the disabled, and fire regulations in relation to buildings and their maintenance;
- educational expertise to keep abreast of developments in curriculum requirements;
- nurturing and caring skills to ensure the good health, welfare and correct dietary needs of students;
- administration skills within the context of understanding the complex interrelationship between the Department for Education and Employment, local education authorities and their educational establishment;
- teamworking skills to ensure the governing body can work in a cohesive and productive way.

On top of all these requirements comes the vital ingredient that those who offer themselves are able to reflect the aspirations and expectations of the community served by the school or college.

Serving on community bodies such as those mentioned above provides anyone with a managerial, supervisory, administrative, technical or caring background with a wonderful opportunity to put their skills into a new context. And while you generate this new interest, you also generate a new network of contacts, build on your own skills base and have the personal satisfaction of doing something which is not just worthwhile with your life, but essential to the well-being of others and to the local community.

Making your social experiences more satisfying

Although socialising is important once you have time to yourself, if it ceases to be a satisfying experience you are actually damaging your interpersonal skills rather than enhancing them. The answer to the rapidly declining satisfaction levels is not necessarily to pull back completely from regular social occasions, but to ease back on them and make space for new dimensions in your life.

You can do this either by putting your socialising into another context where the purpose for meeting people is over and above the socialising itself, for example, by joining a civic society or local action group campaigning for a particular goal; or you can sink yourself into a deeper commitment by taking on regular voluntary work in a charity shop or being involved in a 'Friends' group supporting your local hospital or theatre.

Another option is to join your nearest branch of the University of the Third Age (U3A). There are more than 350 U3As throughout the UK at the moment with a total membership in excess of 65,000. They are self-funded and self-managed organisations with a parent Trust operating from London which receives grants and donations to help it provide a range of support services to branches.

Unlike higher education institutions, the U3A is a learning cooperative where older people with an interest in learning share education, creative and leisure activities. It has members, not students, and you do not need qualifications to join. Branches draw on the knowledge, experience and skills of their members to organise study and activity groups to suit the wishes of their membership. Between the various U3As they offer over 150 topics on a wide range of subjects such as art, foreign languages, music, history, life sciences, literature, poetry, theatre-going, philosophy, world faiths, crafts, field studies, archaeology, bird watching and computing. No qualifications are issued: the emphasis is on the learning experience for its own sake.

If you happen to live in a part of the country where the nearest U3A is beyond reasonable travelling distance, you could even think about taking the initiative yourself and starting up a new branch with the help of the national office.

If you are genuinely stumped for ideas about what you might like to do with your time, you can't do better than trawl through the pages of the local paper. Read the articles which tell you about the personalities and the activities of groups in your area and choose from those where you:

◆   are interested in what the group does;
◆   like the sound of the way they go about things;

♦ feel you would be able to contribute relevant skills to the group if you joined.

You can also study some of the advertisements placed in the forthcoming events section to see if there is anything being organised by a local group which might act as a 'taster' of the group's activities. This gives you the opportunity to meet the people involved without committing yourself before you are really ready to do so.

The secret of success in joining any group is that you should be certain you will be happy committing your time and effort to them. There is nothing worse that being sucked into an organisation too soon and not having the chance to gauge whether your involvement is likely to be to your mutual advantage or not. For a while at least, you need to stay at arm's length to make a proper judgement.

Reusing your parenting skills

There is an increasing need these days for childcare facilities as women return to the workplace. With a much more mobile workforce now, the extended family support network is less likely to be able to step into the breach. There is also the knock-on effect where couples who delay starting their families until their late twenties or early thirties have parents who are much older than their own grandparents were and who are therefore less physically able to care for young children.

But this is not the picture in all cases, and many people find their grandchildren provide them with the opportunity to resurrect parenting skills in later years. Besides the obvious nurturing and caring skills, there are others which can foster children's interests and skills in later life. Take, for example, the following everyday activities where children can take part in what you are doing and learn from your expertise:

♦ tending the garden
♦ feeding and caring for animals
♦ baking or knitting.

Add into these a few more specialised skills that you can demonstrate such as:

- playing a musical instrument
- making a model or toy
- speaking another language
- swimming

and take it from there to include anything and everything you could usefully pass on.

The big advantage of grandparenting skills is that they are probably broader than the range you had to hand when you were a parent yourself, since you may well have acquired new skills since your own children grew up and left home.

Making more of your time alone

If you are in the position of finding yourself at home with your partner and neither of you had bargained for this sudden 24-hour-a-day closeness, friction can develop very quickly.

Planning to set time aside for your personal space and inner renewal may be something you have never given much thought to because while you were working it was part of the working day and happened without you noticing it. Most people have time to themselves while they travel to work: you may have been crammed in an overcrowded bus or train, or had a car full of schoolchildren you were dropping off en route, but the chances are that you were able mentally to cut yourself off from the general hubbub around you and think your own thoughts.

Your new daily schedule may become irksome because you suddenly find you no longer have this mental space. The art of readjustment is to build into your life activities which will allow both of you to share some, but not all, of your time together.

> Knowing how to get pleasure from being on your own is a useful skill in its own right, and no less important than having good social skills.

Almost everyone needs time to be alone but no one wants to feel lonely. For someone who is already living on their own, there will still be the need to feel contented and fulfilled between those periods of socialising or community-based activities. Just as you did when you were at work, you need a proper balance between time with others and time devoted to yourself.

Being able to cope with solitude in a positive way provides a buttress against the time when getting around ceases to be quite so easy as it was in the past and your opportunity to meet people drops away. In the longer term of course, it can also provide a powerful means of overcoming the debilitating effects of grief and loss.

Feeling positive about being on your own is often achieved by simply completing an activity you decided you would like to do. While you are still active this can be quite physical, like decorating the spare room, digging over the vegetable patch or taking the dog for a long walk. It can be less physical, such as designing a new kitchen, completing a jigsaw, or sewing. Or it can be completely relaxing, such as listening to a favourite piece of music, reading a novel or watching TV.

There is also the satisfaction to be had from mentally stimulating activities such as tackling a difficult crossword puzzle, composing haiku, or taking up a course of study using distance learning facilities.

Extending your skills base

Just because you are no longer thinking about having to learn new skills as part of your working life, there is nothing to stop you thinking about doing or learning new and exciting things, just for the personal pleasure these might give you.

Being free from the constraints of the working week gives you the chance to be adventurous. How adventurous, of course, is up to you, but it is not uncommon to meet those who have decided to take on new challenges once they have the time to devote to them. There are those who opt to take flying lessons, or learn scuba diving; those who take up crosscountry skiing or enrol for advanced driving courses; or those who discover archery or latent acting abilities.

If you are not quite so radical in your approach, you may want to pick up old hobbies and take them a step further than you did previously: tackle a more complicated piece of woodwork; use a different painting or drawing medium; take on the challenge of writing a full-length novel instead of short stories; design your own clothes, or try your hand at gourmet cooking. The possibilities are only limited by the hobbies you have had in the past.

Using your brain

As we discussed in Chapter 9, the most important activity to foster is mental activity. There is nothing guaranteed to keep you from mentally deteriorating with the passage of time, but you can do a great deal to stem the tide if you are not suffering from a mentally debilitating illness.

One way is to take a course of study. This is not the same as joining in the activities of the University of the Third Age or enrolling at an adult education centre to take non-vocational courses: this is taking a course of study with the serious intention of completing an examination at the end of it and possibly continuing to study over a period of years for no other reason than that you are interested in the topic and still want to achieve a goal.

Distance learning is the modern generic term for what used to be known as correspondence courses. Providers are strictly monitored by the Open and Distance Learning Quality Council (see Useful Addresses on page 187) to ensure the quality of the courses they offer.

But by far the largest distance learning provider is now The Open University with over 160,000 students worldwide (see Useful Addresses on page 187). The OU provides a bewildering array of courses in the arts, law, education, classical studies, health and social welfare, languages, social sciences, sciences, mathematics, computing, environmental studies and technology, with qualifications at all levels from diplomas and ordinary degrees to higher degrees.

Never has it been so easy to study.

The OU was created to meet the needs of those who cannot attend other higher education institutions because of their personal circumstances. For most courses you don't need any qualifications to join, and you can study at home using the variety of study materials provided – written texts, audio and video cassettes, computer software (where relevant), home experiment kits for science and technology courses – all with the benefit of contact with a personal tutor and a regionally based advisory service.

This format provides the ideal opportunity for you to enjoy the experience of higher education which you may have missed out on earlier in your life. It is borne out by the number of older students who enrol for courses and who in many cases go on to receive their degrees.

What is particularly heartening is that disability is no bar to study. Provision is made for those with impaired hearing or sight to receive their study texts in different formats, and guidance is offered as to what type of hearing or visual aid might be available to overcome other difficulties. For those too far away from tuition centres, tuition can take place over the telephone and special arrangements are made for disabled students to attend the now famous 'Summer Schools'.

Nor are examinations a problem. Any difficulties encountered by someone with physical handicaps are taken into account. If you have a medical or physical problem that makes it impossible for you to take an examination under normal examination conditions, these difficulties are allowed for as part of the examination process. This can include breaks for exercise for those who cannot physically sit for long periods without pain, to allowing more time for those who cannot read quickly because of sight problems. In extreme cases, if there is any medical or physical problem that prevents you from attending the nearest local examination centre, arrangements can be made for you to take your examinations at home under supervision.

If you have ever had a hankering to take up study again, the OU might well meet your needs. But whether you decide to follow a formal course of study or a non-vocational one, keeping mentally alert is something you can do even when mobility becomes more of a problem.

Devising your Third Age Action Plan

A suggested Action Plan format is set out in Worksheet 29 on page 185, but like the Action Plan itself, it is not meant to be prescriptive or cast in tablets of bronze. Now, as at no time in your life before, you can build in your own flexibility to suit your own needs.

Like all action plans, it will need regular revision, updating and reviewing to reflect changes in your circumstances while at the same time providing you with a positive stimulus and sense of purpose.

When it is complete, file it with the rest of your Personal Resource Pack papers and consciously make the effort to reread what you have set down at regular intervals – say monthly or six monthly – and adjust, amend and revise it where necessary.

Worksheet 29: Action Plan for the next half of my life

Things I would like to do now/in ten years/in twenty years etc.

Portable skills I have to do these:

Additional skills I need are:

How can I get these skills?

Review dates (every six months/every year):

What have I achieved?

What would I like to achieve before the next review date?

Refurbishing your life raft

At this stage your life raft is complete, all your valuable life skills recorded, put to some use, used in a different way, built on or used again at a later date.

Right at the start of the process of building the raft it was stressed how important it was to keep reminding yourself just how many life skills you had in your possession. By the time you completed all your skills audits, the range and scope of your talents should have become clear enough to show you that regardless of what stage you are in your life, there are still opportunities to seize and adventures to embark on.

Occasionally ask yourself: do I want to achieve something more – can I add another skills plank to my raft? Then see if you can – and set off on a new and exciting journey.

Thinking Slot 20

- Describe yourself using as many of your skills as you can think of.
- How does this description compare with the one you compiled for Thinking Slot 8 (page 20)?

Summary

This final chapter looked at how you can give more meaning to the second half of your life beyond the world of work.

- You were given tips on avoiding boredom, facing up to financial limitations, infirmity and possible ill-health.
- You were encouraged to set about doing something constructive to maintain the quality of your life.
- Options you could consider included taking your skills into the community, making social experiences more satisfying, reusing parenting skills as grandparents and making time on your own an enjoyable experience.
- Alternative courses of action were suggested to extend your skills base, including returning to formal study to maintain mental activity regardless of age or infirmity.
- You were asked to devise a personal Action Plan to cover the second half of your life to include what you wanted to do and how you would go about achieving your goals.

Useful Addresses

Centre for Continuing Education, Training and Development
(CETAD), Lancaster University, Bailrigg, Lancaster LA1 4AZ.
Tel: (01524) 593318, Fax: (01524) 593319
E-mail: cetad@lancaster.ac.uk
Website: www.lancs.ac.uk/users/cetad

Open and Distance Learning Quality Council, Westminster
Central Hall, Storey's Gate, London SW1H 9NH
Tel: (020) 7233 3466

The Open University, PO Box 71, Milton Keynes MK7 6AG
Tel: (01908) 274066, Fax: (01908) 653744
Helpline (between 5–9 p.m. Mon–Fri): (0541) 596953
Website: http://www.open.ac.uk/

Qualifications and Curriculum Authority, 27 Bolton Street,
London W1Y 7PD.
Tel: (020) 7509 5555

The University of the Third Age, 26 Harrison Street, London
WC1H 8JG.
Tel: (020) 7837 8838, Fax: (020) 7837 8845
E-mail: national.office@u3a.org.uk
Website: http://u3a.org.uk

Recommended Reading

Perfect People Skills: Andrew Acland (Arrow Books) 1997, UK
What Color is Your Parachute? Richard Bolles (Ten Speed) 1999
edition
Good Retirement Guide: Rosemary Brown (Kogan Page) 1996, UK
The Which? Guide to Active Retirement: The Consumer
Association 1997, UK
Learning Exam Skills: Hy Cumper, P McVea (Blackstone) 1996,
UK
The Chance to Live More Than Once: Barry Curnow & John
McLean Fox (Management Books 2000) 1996, UK
Tactics: Edward de Bono (HarperCollins) 1985, UK
Help!: Hazel Evans (Pan) 1996, UK
Developing your Employment Skills: Valerie Foster (Trotman) 1998,
UK
Growing Old Disgracefully: The Hen Co-op (Crossing Press) 1994,
USA
Build Your Own Rainbow: Barrie Hopson (Lifeskills Associates)
1989, UK
Feel the Fear and Do it Anyway: Susan Jeffers (Arrow) 1991, UK
Improving Study Skills: Conrad Lashley (Cassell) 1995, UK
Go for it!: Martyn Lewis (Queen Anne Press) 1996, UK
The 110% Solution: Mark McCormack Audio Cassette (Random
House Audiobooks) 1992
Superlife: Anne Naylor (Thorsons) 1992, UK
Women Returning to Higher Education: Gillian Pascall (Open
University) 1993, UK
Women Returners' Guide: Linda Stoker (Bloomsbury) 1991, UK
30 Minutes to Boost your Communication Skills: Elizabeth Tierney
(Kogan Page) 1997, UK

Index